TALES FROM THE TRENCHES

TALES FROM THE TRENCHES

ADVICE FOR NEW REAL ESTATE AGENTS

BILL GIANNINI
Realtor®
Platinum Real Estate Professionals
Las Vegas, NV

FIRST EDITION

Copyright © 2018 by Bill Giannini

All rights reserved. No part of this book may be reproduced in any form or by any electrical or mechanical means, including photocopying, or by any information storage or retrieval system without permission in writing from the publisher/author, except by a reviewer who may quote brief passages under Fair Use law.

ISBN 10: 1984914030
ISBN 13: 9781984914033

This book is about my experiences and lessons learned while working with countless different clients and agents. Many of these situations have been similar in discourse, circumstance, and outcome. No one has been mentioned by name.

Contents

UGH 1
1. IT'S NOT A JOB, IT'S A LIFESTYLE 5
QUALIFY 7
WHEN THE UNIVERSE IS TALKING TO YOU 10
A FRAGILE LUXURY 14
SHUT UP, ALREADY 16
THIRD WHEEL 20
THE LEAD... 28
2. TIME IS MONEY 35
REAL ESTATE UNIT #5387691 37
THE TRUTH OF THE MATTER 40
HOW MUCH YOU GOT? 44
HASTE NOT WASTE 48
CHECK THE SCHEDULE.. 53
MAYBE WE CAN'T AFFORD THAT NOW 57
OPEN FOR BUSINESS 62
WHAT WAS THAT ABOUT A PAPERLESS SOCIETY? 66
3. IT'S A PEOPLE BUSINESS 73
NOT YOUR GRANDPA'S REAL ESTATE AGENT 75
DO UNTO OTHERS 81
DON'T BE A DICK 88
YOU CAN'T ALWAYS GET WHAT YOU WANT 94
BE SAFE 103
4. HOW DOES IT WORK? 107
LISA'S ESCROW.. 109
THE OTHER SIDE OF UGH 137

UGH

I just had a client text me and cancel on a big deal.
    Actually two deals.
    He was going to sell his home and buy another. The classic twosome, or "two-fer".
    But no. Cancelling.
    Fifteen grand in commission out the window.
    Are you serious?
    Life of a real estate agent.

Sure, I didn't need that money to survive, but I could've found good ways to use some of it.
    Maybe pay down some credit cards.
    Maybe get a canopy for my backyard.
    Maybe take a short trip with my girlfriend.
    I don't know. All this, of course, after putting away some for the taxman. Client was very apologetic, sorry for the time I'd already spent researching the market for him and showing him the homes he requested to see. This is part of the game. Get them excited. Show them what they could have. Pull them in!
    Mark's a good guy. I was happy to do it. I've known him about nine years now. We worked together in the same drug retail outfit. When I got into real estate I sold him his first house, the one he was just planning to sell.

His reason for pulling out is personal and I understand it. He's financially capable. He's motivated to find a newer, bigger home. But he's just not quite ready yet, not quite there. So I won't push him. I won't assault him with reasons why he should reconsider, or try to convince him to move forward and that he'll be glad he did it in the end. No. Because I'd like to maintain a relationship with him. It's easy to lose people if you're too pushy. I want him to contact me again if he ever changes his mind. And he says he will. I'll be the first one he calls. And I like to believe that. I've been burned before. But I don't think it'll happen with Mark.

Ultimately my livelihood depends upon people's whims. Practical strangers' whims, a lot of the time.

My potential income fluctuates with individual clients' moods.

That's a crazy concept to most people who depend on a steady reliable income each week, each month. I've learned to accept it.

You can't be a full-time agent if you can't accept that.
Like a downed boxer, you have get back up off the mat.

Another $15K in commission may be coming your way and you don't even know it yet. The phone rings while you're watching TV. A text or email appears while you're at dinner. Boom! You're back on track. Maybe that'll happen to me. My feelers are out everywhere. I have irons in the fire. I have lovely past clients who surprise me with wonderful referrals. Maybe one of those will light up my phone any moment. And then perhaps my old friend Mark will think again and decide he wants to buy and sell after all. Cool, he's back in the game. Plus I got that other new one to jump on. This happens.

That's why I'm still an agent, and why I'm ok with things whenever I feel momentarily...screwed.

#REALESTATEAGENTLIFE – or something like that.

1. IT'S NOT A JOB, IT'S A LIFESTYLE

QUALIFY

I'm often asked what it takes to become an agent. People are very curious about it.

It's not difficult.

It doesn't require a college degree. There's no special training needed. You just need an attention span, plus some endurance and drive.

First there's a 90-hour course, covering everything from contracts to ethics to taxes to construction terms. Two thirds of it is national, the same stuff any student across the United States is tested on. The rest pertains to your specific state.

If your state is okay with it, you can take your course online. Some require classroom training only. That's a bummer if you're working another job in the meantime. I was fortunate that Nevada accepts the online option, so I could toil at the store in the daytime and evenings and work on my coursework late at night. I worked at my own pace, absorbing and testing myself on the material along the way. It took me six months.

You have to be able to get through those 90 hours of stuff. Much of it's not very exciting. Pretty boring, actually. But without it, there's no moving forward to the next step.

The exam.

This really made me nervous. I wanted to pass it so bad. I *had* to pass it. I'd already told all my family and friends I was doing it. I couldn't imagine crawling back and telling them I'd failed.

You find out your results immediately. That very day. There's no waiting. It's all computerized and your score is ready for you as soon as you leave the testing room. It all comes down to that moment. Sure, you can take the test again. You can take it over and over. But you also have to pay the fee over and over. I believe it was somewhere around $150. Who wants to do that?

Here's how I did.

The testing center was downtown, at least a 30-minute drive from my house. The exam was scheduled for 9 AM. My wife at the time suggested I get a hotel room nearby and spend the night there in order to make my morning easier and less stressed. Super idea. I am still thankful to her for it. I got a room about five minutes away from the test site. There was a Starbucks right down the street. Perfect.

In my room that night I went over my thick binders of course material a few more times until a voice told me, "That's it. Stop. Enough. You're ready."

I ate light, a chicken salad. Slept wonderfully.

In the morning, charged by caffeine, I got to the place in plenty of time, went into a big dim room full of tables and cubbies, and took my seat. Several clicks later I had the first test question in front of me, the first of 120. Did I freeze a bit? Yes.

Had I studied enough?

Was I going to fail?

Was I a fraud?

Oh man, those first few answers were tough decisions. But then I started to relax. Concentration kicked in. Turned out I knew more than I thought I did. I completed the exam in the allotted time, careful not to second-guess myself on too many questions. In three hours I was done.

I left the room feeling kind of numb. My eyes were strained from the bright monitor. My hand was stiff from gripping the mouse. I feared I hadn't done as well as I'd hoped. A calm, unassuming middle-aged lady was seated at a desk and I sat down in front of her. She handed me a piece of paper with my results on it. I dared glance at it....

Holy crap. I'd succeeded. Ninety-one percent. An A-.

For someone who'd been a poor test taker in high school and college, this totally blew me away. I'd worked hard and earned myself a new career!

I generously thanked the desk lady as if she'd had something to do with it and flew out the door into the sunny day. I thought of how F. Scott Fitzgerald had run out in the street between cars in celebration, announcing he'd landed a publishing contract for his first novel. That's how I felt. I didn't run into the street but I got into my car and probably drove too fast.

Not until I actually became an agent did I realize an ironic truth. I would use practically nothing from that exam ever again.

WHEN THE UNIVERSE IS TALKING TO YOU

I could've stayed in retail. Could've stayed there, toiling, sweating, accomplishing a lot and yet nothing. Ten years I spent as a supervisor/key carrier/assistant manager in two major drug store chains.

In case you don't know, this is how those stores work.

You get one major weekly delivery – "truck" or "load" – and you spend the rest of the week putting the product away and placing orders for the next one.

In the meantime you manage the employees, help the customers, and keep the whole operation rolling. It's supposed to be a team effort, of course, but not all teams work well together. Some team members don't work at all. Maybe you've known one. Or been one!

Then every year, some invisible people referred to as "corporate bean-counters" slash your usable labor hours just a bit more, so you're forced to do more with less. The job remains the same, but the workforce is reduced. Stress levels are raised. The pay raises are negligible. It's like trying to squeeze the last remaining juice out of an orange. If you've ever known anyone who works retail, you've probably heard this complaint before. Honestly, it's deflating for anyone involved.

During extra busy weeks, like around holidays, trucks often don't get completely put away, which means that shelves remain unfilled and the business loses sales. And sales are what it's all about.

Stockholders.

Earnings.

You know how it is. Competition. The results are never enough. The corporate expectations are too high. It's just greed. But you have no option other than to just roll with it.

It was amazing the number of steps I used to walk in a day. Out of curiosity I now wish I'd used a pedometer. Between the stockroom, the office, the front end of the store, the pharmacy in the backend, even the parking lot, I was like a ping pong ball, fairly nonstop for 8 hours a day. I can't say it didn't keep me in shape.

I used to tell my co-managers that if an average person came in off the street and had to follow us around, shadow us, for an entire shift, they'd be on the floor long before the end of the day.

You go home sweaty and sore and pretty wound-up from buzzing around all day. Hopefully all went well with the job and you didn't have any employee or customer issues that may haunt you the next time you walk through the door. Those are great for messing with your relaxation at home and maybe even your sleep. And over what? A mispriced item? A refused refund? An argument with a lazy cashier? Had them all.

Over time, this pressure cooker atmosphere starts to wear you down like the lead of a pencil. The job isn't easy. It's easy on paper. Yet when you throw real human beings and a merciless clock into the equation, it's hard to add it all up. I was good. I took my duties seriously. The many store managers I worked under in ten years all loved having me around because I made their jobs just that much easier. Even though they made more money, I didn't want their job because I knew they had to face the full punishment of higher management. Shit rolls downhill, yes, but I didn't want to be the one on the frontline taking it squarely in the face.

There was one weak moment when I took a test to try and move up to the rank above me, just below the store manager. My heart wasn't in it. I didn't study enough. I failed. That was a sign. I could've taken it again, but I no longer wanted to.

Why try to get promoted closer to a position I didn't want? It made no sense.

After that I began to realize I couldn't do this forever. My body wouldn't take it, plus I was tired of being frustrated daily by those below and above me in rank. The hours were bad as well. Every week a different schedule. I couldn't plan anything. I was unhappy. I'd go home grumpy. Uptight. Certain aspects of the job I still liked. But the negative stuff, the orange-squeezing stuff, it was getting to me. I guess I wanted more control of my life. I needed a whole new career. I started studying for my real estate license. During that time I met my future mentors through a Craigslist ad for some furniture.

My wife and I had purchased a new home and were planning to rent our old one. We had a fine old dining room set from the 1960s that just wasn't going to make it, style-wise, in the new place, so I listed it for sale. I got an email response from some lady and noticed that her signature stated she was a Realtor®.

How interesting, I thought, that's what I want to be!

I answered the ad and she showed up at the house with her husband, also an agent. They loved the dining set. I happened to mention I was looking to get licensed in real estate. They latched onto me right away.

"When you get licensed, come work with us," they chimed.

Wow, I already had a job. It would be a forty-five minute drive to their office, but so what, I was in, just like that. I couldn't argue it. What an incentive to get my coursework done and pass that exam!

We stayed in touch and they invited my wife and me to their company Christmas party.

It was a regal affair. Giant hall, classy band, great food, open bar, happily lit people, we had it all. An aura of money permeated the air. I'd never been to such a glitzy party before. How come the stores didn't do anything like this at the holidays? They were billion-dollar operations!

At our table I was lavished over by team leaders and coaches who couldn't welcome me enough to the exciting world of real estate -- and here I was, still only a prospect, not even licensed yet. I was being wined and dined to the fullest and didn't even realize it. My wife didn't appreciate how touchy the women were with me. I felt like a complete outsider yet lured in. What a contrast to the sweaty, thankless world of retail.

I'd found my new gig, partly in thanks to an innocent Craigslist ad.

I worked with that lovely couple as part of their team for almost five years before branching out on my own.

That good old furniture set still sits in their dining room today.

A FRAGILE LUXURY

Most real estate agents are part-time. They have a regular job providing regular income and only put on their sales hat if something comes up. A family member wants to sell or buy, or a friend, maybe a co-worker. Everyone knows an agent or two, and people want to use who they know and trust. I knew I'd have to do more than that. I couldn't stay in retail and do real estate only occasionally. I needed to jump in completely.

In Clark County, where I work, 85% of agents are part-time. That means 15% are full-time.

We'll call them the 15er's and the 85er's.

The 15er's try to steer potential buyers and sellers away from the 85er's. They claim they're not really dedicated and may be out of touch with the realities of the market, unlike someone who's immersed in it every day.

I see why the 85er's do it. They feel this is a way to make some extra cash on the side from time to time and still keep the security of a biweekly or monthly paycheck. I understand it. Whereas the 15er's are the ones who made the plunge. Perhaps they gave up another stable, paycheck-earning career to start their own business and work for themselves. Or perhaps they found themselves stranded, between careers, and decided, "Screw that, I'll be my own boss and make my own hours and improve my life!"

It takes quite a commitment, and drive, and passion, to do that. There's no safety net. You have to succeed or else. Make that commission or maybe don't pay the mortgage. That's the difference between the 85er's and the 15er's.

At my first company, as a new recruit, I was told that real estate is not a job, it's a lifestyle.

It really is. As a 15er, I have no timeclock. There's no manager watching over me. I create my own work and tackle whatever comes along with it. I get up in the morning, brew some coffee, and go straight to it. When I'm done or need a break, I go do something else. My time, my responsibility.

My accountability for my own successes or failures.

I've known some agents to close a property, receive a sizable commission check, and then disappear for a month, like they're on an instant vacation. That's fine, they can do whatever they like. But I laugh when they come back and have no escrows to work on and are running out of money.

Consistency counts.

"Always keep your pipeline full," you'll hear.

"ABC, Always Be Closing." Have you seen *Glengarry Glen Ross*?

I took control and chose to live the lifestyle.

A 15er all the way. Even though it's not always as easy as some people may think.

SHUT UP, ALREADY

The lifestyle of always being "on", of constantly being on the lookout for prospects, is a tough one to adjust to in the beginning.

It's like how actors taking on a role in a film have to *become* that character.

While you're in training, your coach, team leader, or whomever you're under will say, "Start with your sphere."

That's your family and friends, co-workers, teachers, dentist, ex, anyone who may be lurking in your contacts list. You're probably envisioning them all right now, even the ones you don't like that much (yes, you should talk to them too).

Who in that group may want to buy or sell a home? That's the question you set out to ask when you gather up those names and start making phone calls. They're your "sphere", so they'll surely want to help you get your real estate career off the ground, right?

Keep in mind, you're not selling jeans here. You're selling dreams and investments costing hundreds of thousands of dollars. Millions maybe. It may take a whole lot of persuasion.

Everyone is thrilled to hear from you. And then you bring up the real motive for your call.

"So, as you know, I'm new in real estate and I was wondering.... Are you considering selling your home?" Or, "Or have you thought about buying a house?"

You're nervous and clumsy on the phone. You have none of the easy smoothness that comes with years of experience in dealing with buyers and sellers. You've seen no real estate trends or market ups-and-downs. You've got no answers to lending- or escrow-related questions. You're just a dressed-up guy or girl in an office cubicle desperately trying to make your first sale off your Uncle Ted.

Uncle Ted says he might be looking to sell in six months, maybe a year.

Good, you have a lead, a prospective sale to follow up on.

It's sketchy and long-term, but it's a lead.

You BS a little more and finally tell him you have a meeting coming up and have to get off the phone. You note it down:

"Call Ted in 3 mos."

Then you move on to the next name in the list -- Ahmad, the pharmacist from the drugstore where you used to work. He's a cool guy, and a pharmacist, so he'll probably want to buy something nice and expensive. Good sale there. Good commission.

Oh, he's not answering. Well, leave him a message. He'll get back to you. He's probably busy counting little white pills.

Next.

You spend your entire morning doing this. By lunch you've made good headway. No commitments yet, but a lot of prospects. A maybe's better than a no, you tell yourself. You feel good about things. You talked with real live people about real estate, your new industry. And they didn't hang up on you, because they knew you.

You'll do the rest tomorrow morning. More training classes this afternoon.

You never imagine that six months down the line, you could be feeling a bit discouraged by the fact that no one in your digital rolodex has come through for you.

They all want to see you succeed, but again, remember, what you're trying to sell them involves one of the biggest and most important decisions of their lives. People will get to this point when they're ready, willing, and able. Getting you your first commission check is not their prime concern. They don't mean to desert you. They're just not ready for you. You don't realize you may come across as trying to stuff it down their throat.

You could get lucky. Undoubtedly this approach works sometimes. You never know who's looking to buy or sell. Which is why you're supposed to ask *everybody*.

If your sphere fails you, you've got to reach out. To *everybody*. That's what your coaches will tell you.

Good advice. But believe me, it can get nauseating.

When I was a new agent, I'd go out for evening walks with my wife around our subdivision. We'd only lived there six months and were still running into folks we hadn't met.

We would see someone new and introduce ourselves. You know, the neighborly thing. But I wasn't just any neighbor. I was a shark looking for blood.

"I'm a Realtor®," I would proclaim.

"Oh." Their mood and tone would instantly change. Not for the better.

"Do you know you anyone looking to buy or sell?"

"Uh, not at this time."

"Well okay, here's one of my cards."

Woah.

Who's this new sales guy working our street? Watch out for him!

I did it to them all.

In high school, if you ask too many girls out to the prom and get turned down repeatedly, sooner or later all the girls in the school get to know who you are and you'd best look for your date elsewhere. Not that that happened to me or anything, I'm just saying....

My neighborly solicitations frustrated my wife, who actually at one time had indeed chosen to date me. She said I needed to chill out, that I was chasing everyone away. But she didn't understand – I was only doing what I was programmed to do. No one else I knew was buying or selling. So I had to carefully lurk, then pounce. I had to be the shark.

To this day, a very nice lady who lives near one of my relatives will hardly even look at me, she's so afraid I'm about to ask her to sell her house. Which I know she won't, so I won't ask. Lovely lady, but I scarred her somehow. Too aggressive at the start.

I'm better at this now. I've learned how to work real estate more casually into conversations. I still chat with a lot of strangers but not everyone I meet. Perhaps I'm losing the occasional opportunity, but you get to be good at reading the situation you're in. You get a feeling. Just like other things in life. Such as knowing when, or when not, to make a joke or comment on something. Or like choosing fights. People give out those vibes, good or bad. You've got to listen to your gut.

The crazy thing is, everyone is interested in real estate. If they own a home, they want to know what it's worth and how the local market's doing. If they're renting, they want to know when they'd be able to buy and what it's going to take. They're all hungry for real estate news and how it pertains to them.

They just don't always seem to want to hear it from you or me.

THIRD WHEEL

Agents aren't always particularly liked.

We tend to get lumped in with lawyers and car salesmen. Some people like to think we make too much money and do nothing. They don't trust us because they believe we're only out for the sale.

It's true we do want the sale. We want the commission check. But we also want happy clients. At least I do. Happy clients often give referrals, which leads to more business. I say "often" due to the fact that I've had many happy clients who I never hear from again after closing. So strange. So strange is the client-agent relationship.

It's created out of thin air, this relationship. One day a buyer is nothing but a name and a number in a text message. The next day you're meeting him or her, or them, and touring houses with them.

Strangers.

My mother taught me not to talk to them, but I've long since broken that rule. If the idea of small talk with someone you've never met before frightens or repels you, this isn't the field for you. Sometimes you'll have strangers in your own car speaking amongst themselves in a language you don't understand. You'll have to accept that. They probably aren't talking about you. They may be arguing over their budget or commenting on a house you just showed them. Or maybe they *are* talking about you. Who cares? It's just part of the job. You smile and remain polite and professional. Geez, you don't have to live with them after you sell them a house!

Buying or selling a home is a topsy-turvy, emotional experience. If you've ever done it, you know. Even if you haven't done it, you know how excited you get at the prospect of owning your own home, or how dejected you feel if for some reason you can't.

As an agent, you will undoubtedly become an unwitting therapist for your buyer or seller at some point in the process. That is, you may become the sounding board or the shoulder to cry on for someone you didn't even know two months ago. And they get emotional. And stressed out. Some little, or big, thing can always go wrong during an escrow. A good agent must be ready and able to handle the fallout.

I've had to figuratively talk my clients out of trees and off ledges many times. I've had to explain away unpleasant surprises in calm, logical terms with a soothing gravity. I suppose my ten years in retail management got me good at that. When you basically have strangers in your face all day, day after day, you learn about personalities and how to deal with all different kinds of them. Some require more finesse. Some are more straightforward.

Just like how some folks barely even read important paperwork before signing, while others go over every line.

It takes patience to work with people. All sorts of people. You must have a therapeutic bone in you to do this. You must be able to sit them down on the couch. You can't walk away. I mean, you could, but then there goes your deal, and maybe your reputation too.

Sometimes they're really nice people. Especially couples. You jabber away and find out interesting things about them. You see them again and again. Maybe meet their kids or parents. You're their agent, the licensed professional with the magical key to their future. They laugh with you, complain to you, take the ups and downs of realty with you.

You may even start to think, "I like these people. I could hang out with them."

Of course you maintain your professionalism. You are, after all, not only working with them but *for* them. They could easily fire you. Cut you out of their life. You wouldn't want that.

You do your best to keep them satisfied and sane throughout the buying or selling process. I strive to keep as much stress as possible out of my clients' lives. Any good agent would. Any little catastrophes or problems come up, I try to resolve them if I can without bothering the clients and upsetting them. This takes research. And timing. And tact. And diplomacy. Agents do a lot, let me tell you.

Backstage it may be chaos, but the show goes on.

Months go by and finally it's time to close. The sale is almost complete. You're all buddies by now, your clients and you. Through good and bad you got it done and stuck together. They trusted you; you guided them. Everyone's feeling good. You sit together in the signing room and reflect on things as if you've known each other for years.

"Remember when we almost thought our deal was dead?"

That kind of stuff. It's all laughable at this point.

It's especially emotional with buyers. Sellers can be emotional as well, but they're more like, "Ok, where's my money?"

Buyers have a new place to call home.

Once the house closes, I enjoy meeting my buyers there and handing them their keys (or key). It's very satisfying. It gives closure to what you've just been through together.

But oddly enough, it usually gives closure to the relationship as well.

With a shaky hand they turn that key and open the door. They walk in. It's their property now. This place they've been chasing, hunting, for a month, maybe two, maybe six or more, it's theirs. Suddenly you're not just an agent, you're a visitor. Their adrenaline is pumping and they're ready to get started on things. They don't need you anymore.

After all the hugs and handshakes and congratulations settle down, you're standing there, kind of in their way.

I was watching a show on HGTV and saw this exact situation unfold.

The buyers said to the agent jokingly, "OK, now get out of our house!"

They all laughed, but there was a twinge of seriousness in that comment.

Last year I finished up working with a guy and his wife, repeat clients. Really nice couple, great people. My team and I had previously aided them in selling their first home and buying their second. Now I'd sold their second and got them into their third.

Towering over me in his new family room, this huge guy shakes my hand and proclaims in a weary tone, "Well Bill, after this I hope I never have to see you again."

I know he meant he hoped he wouldn't have to buy or sell any more houses and that he was there to stay. But in the moment it stunned me hearing those words, put that very way.

Despite my occasional texts or emails, I haven't heard from him or his wife since.

That relationship, once so heated in the rush and fury of a real estate transaction, turned ice cold immediately. Severed, like a finger or limb. It happens all the time. New agents have to adjust to it.

My old team leader Tim was fantastic at short sales. He performed over a hundred of them. We always say there's nothing short about a short sale. They take months, sometimes years. The banks will take forever to respond to offers, and everyone involved – buyer, seller, both agents, whomever else – is forced to wait. Often when the banks do respond, it's with news that they want more money for the property. Highly frustrating. If you've ever purchased a short sale or sold one, you know how it can be.

Well, Tim can be an impatient guy, but he knew how to find the extra will and tenacity to get these difficult transactions to the finish line. In doing so he helped a lot of people, saving them from foreclosure or bankruptcy, shielding them from complete financial ruin. And then, like the wind, so many of them were gone.

"These short sale clients, you do so much for them, and then you never hear from them again!" he would lament. "No referrals, nothing."

As agents we're accessories. We're vessels. We make it possible for clients to navigate mysterious escrows and achieve what they're after: a purchase or a sale.

Along the way we may sense a friendship building, or at least a pleasant camaraderie. Yet you don't really know what people are thinking. You may think they like you – and usually they do on some level or they wouldn't work with you – but don't assume it will last beyond the transaction.

Several years ago I was working with some buyers I met at an open house. They were a couple near retirement age but still with a few years to go at their jobs. They wanted to find a home closer to work.

We got to know each other well over several months of house hunting. Almost every weekend we'd get together. They treated me like a son, and I really enjoyed their company. At first they were hesitant to make offers, as if they feared they'd buy the wrong house and then see something better come up and regret it. Meanwhile they were passing up homes they really seemed to like. I encouraged them to jump in, to at least try. After six months they finally landed a place they just loved in one of their favorite subdivisions, a mid-century modern neighborhood only minutes from their respective offices. It was just what they wanted.

I thought.

Near the end of the escrow period, only days from closing, I sensed something was wrong. They seemed unhappy. I could tell they wanted out. They were about to be trapped in their new house. The carefree days of touring homes would be over. What if something nicer came on the market and they couldn't have it? Ahhh!

They zeroed in on a small repair that the seller hadn't gotten done in a timely enough manner and demanded to be let out of the contract. I told they'd lose their earnest money deposit (quite a good sum) if they cancelled. Hearing this made them freeze in horror. They didn't want to lose the money. The house would soon be theirs. In their minds they'd been duped, lured in, entrapped.

And somehow I had caused this to happen.

They ended up closing, reluctantly, practically under duress.

We never spoke again. No more Saturday fun. I'd been disowned!

After I got divorced – that's a long story not related to over-zealous real estate activities – I found a new girlfriend and she moved in with me. I was working with a couple who, it turned out, had pretty strong beliefs about marriage. Again, lovely people. They were selling their home and upgrading to something bigger and better. I genuinely enjoyed seeing them each time we met. They seemed to enjoy seeing me.

One day we were viewing a property, and my new living arrangement came up. They were taken aback to learn that I was living with my girlfriend, who obviously was not my wife.

Awkward.

We got past it and remained friendly and got our work together successfully completed.

Had I become the very personification of a sinner in their minds? Had this stained their perception of me? Maybe. Was I a bad person? Of course not. Was I the sort of person they were comfortable associating with in their private, post-real estate lives? Perhaps not.

I don't hear from them anymore.

Did I get paid?

Yes.

Did they get what they wanted?

Yes.

End of transaction, end of relationship. Onto the next one.

For an agent, staying in touch is vital. People might not remember you otherwise. Not everyone is good about storing phone numbers and keeping their contacts organized. Certainly it's easier today than it used to be, you would think. Yet so many times, I've seen agents stung when finding out that Sam Client just listed the house they sold him three years ago with another agent.

Did they keep in touch with Sam? Had it been two years since their last text, phone call, or email correspondence? If so, the agent failed. He or she can't rely on Sam to keep in contact. Sam has other things to do. That's not his job. It's his agent's job.

Little things like personalized calendars, keychains, notepads, coffee mugs, or refrigerator magnets are useful as gifts to clients because they keep you "front of mind" with them. This goes for any kind of business. Why should real estate be any different? You'll always need sales, month after month, year after year.

A coach I knew once stated that fifty good clients will carry you through your real estate career.

These are your fans. They absolutely love you and refer you out any chance they get. You're locked in. And it's sure sweet when those referrals pop up out of nowhere. Take care of those golden fifty, if you get that many. Or those golden hundred, if you're really that good. They're there for you. Just keep them happy.

The problem is, most agents don't have fifty. They're probably lucky to have ten.

So they have to work on everyone. Especially the one-off's. One sale and that's it. Never hear from them again. What happens there?

Maybe they're just satisfied where they are and don't want any sales info or calls.

Or maybe they hated your guts the entire time.

My advice is simple. Don't expect to be liked by everyone, and don't be troubled when your agent-client relationships seem to fall apart or dissolve.

And it's true: not everyone can work with everyone all the time. There are times when it just doesn't work. That's when you refer your problem client out to another agent who may match them better, and hope they close them so you can salvage 25% of the commission for your trouble.

Personal associations based on money issues can be precarious.

And wasn't it really all about money in the first place?

THE LEAD

You can't get these clients, these pseudo-friends, if they don't first show up as leads. Leads must be found, sought out, sweated out. They're the lifeblood of your business, the fuel of your lifestyle.

If you don't work on a team with a team leader who doles them out to you, you'll have to search them out your own, like looking for food on a deserted island.

Years ago I saw a list of ways for agents to find leads, and one of the suggestions was to check the daily obituaries and hang out around mortuaries. It makes sense, but really? Are you going to do that? That sounds like a real estate agent out of a cheesy movie. You don't want to be him. There are plenty of other, less slimy, methods of finding business.

I once approached a house with a moving truck out front. Someone was in the process of loading it up. The front door of the house was wide open. I rang the bell and knocked on the door.

"Be right there!" a man called out from upstairs.

He came down, a guy in his mid-forties, dressed in an old T-shirt and jeans. I introduced myself and asked if he was selling his home.

"Nah, I'm just gonna give it back to the bank."

"Why?"

"Can't sell it."

"Ever consider a short sale?"

"Nah, I'm done."

We spoke a few minutes more and exchanged contact info.

About eight months later, my team completed his short sale. If I hadn't turned down that street and seen the truck, we would've never had that sale. It was luck, paired with a bit of persuasion.

Several more times over the next few years, through good timing, I met homeowners on their driveways and made clients out of them, which led to sales. The reason I was out there anyway was because I was door-knocking, which is my own favorite method of lead-generating. Not only do you get your required exercise, you get to meet potential clients face to face and have a real conversation without them hanging up on you, which happens a lot with cold-calling, the choice of many other agents.

I can't say I haven't had a few doors shut in my face, which I guess is equivalent to being hung-up on, but hey, nothing works every time.

During the dark days of the Great Recession, I did a lot of door-knocking. I went to properties that had been served default notices by mortgage companies or banks. The owners were in danger of impending foreclosure.

At the door I'd speak with them, remind them of what they were facing, and ask if they'd like to sell to avoid foreclosure. I landed a lot of listings this way.

It was also, I admit, a dangerous way of lead-generating. Approaching desperate angry people on their property isn't an easy thing to do.

I could usually tell when I drove up to a place if there could be potential trouble. One dark blue house had concrete gargoyles and satanic statues along its front path, in amongst overgrown shrubbery. Behind a black iron-wrought gate stood an old wooden door nailed over with handwritten wooden signs essentially warning visitors to stay away.

I didn't bother to test it. I took some photos of the statuary and later showed them to a lady at my office.

Her eyes got big and she gasped. "Oh wow, that's a devil house."

At another house I met this tall intense-looking guy who spoke really slowly. His eyes pierced me uncomfortably as I gave him my pitch about helping him sell. All this at the front door.

"Why don't you come inside?" he said.

I knew at once I shouldn't go in there. At least not alone.

"Let me come back tomorrow with my business partner," I suggested. "We can go over everything then."

He said he wouldn't be home. So I took his phone number – the number he gave me – and left.

It turned out to be a bad number. And honestly, I didn't really want to see that guy again anyway.

Curt, another homeowner, I met out on his front porch. He was different in that he had about $50,000 equity in his home. Most of the other ones were underwater and needed to do short sales. He'd fallen behind on his payments and now the bank was after him.

He had an 80's Jheri curl and a really foul mouth, but he listened to my spiel and asked a lot of questions. I was able to cut through his skepticism enough for him to give me his phone number and even invite me in to see the place. I didn't feel too creeped out to refuse. Seemed like a possible listing in the making. Pool house in Vegas!

What a mess. Dim from dark curtains. Cigarette stench. Stains on walls and carpet. Piles of clothes and books everywhere. Chairs stacked on top of couches. TV on with no one watching it. Hot, cluttered, claustrophobic.

That potential $50K equity would be taking a hit.

We passed through the family room to the dining room, then slipped by the gross kitchen out to the backyard.

The pool looked okay. At least it wasn't green, which I'd kind of expected. Curt seemed proud of it.

We sat in old faded lawn chairs and picked up our conversation. Yet suddenly the subject had changed. Curt decided he'd rather rant about his ex-wife and politics, and how real estate agents were always trying to screw him. He got louder and louder.

I repeated, I *emphasized*, that he had profit in the house and that if he failed to act, the bank would seize the property and snatch that profit away from him. I could find a buyer for him fast, get him his cash, and keep him out of foreclosure.

It was like he didn't even hear me. As he got more aggravated I started to think about my exit.

"I gotta go," I said, standing up. "I have an appointment."

"Oh, so now I'm not good enough for ya, huh?"

I headed back in and made a beeline toward the family room. He followed behind me muttering, "I understand, I understand."

He got really close as I opened the front door.

I managed to squeeze outside and say something like, "Let me know if you wanna get together on the house, I can help."

"Yeah, fine."

He slammed the door.

I never sold Curt's house.

I look back and wonder what could've happened in those situations. If I'd gone up the path to the devil house, or stepped inside with the piercing-eyed slow-talker, or stayed with Curt and let him get even angrier....

The point is that I followed my instinct and didn't give myself a chance to find out. Which I believe was the right thing to do. C'mon, no mere listing is worth your health or your life.

While door-knocking or entering on someone's property, you never know who's going to open that door or approach you, and I had my share of little scares throughout the years. But I was bold enough to be there, so maybe I had it coming. Most agents in my area weren't doing this, going straight to distressed homeowners and confronting them with their financial problems. I know it was risky. Profitable but risky.

The one thing I learned early and quick was to make sure I was talking to the homeowner.

At one of the default properties I encountered a thirty-something guy lifting weights in an open garage. He seemed very interested as to why I was there. I assumed he was the owner. As I went into detail about the overdue mortgage and the possible consequences, I came to realize he knew nothing about it. His father had passed and the owner was now his mother, who wasn't home. He said he would speak with her about it later.

That evening I got an angry voicemail from the mother:

"Uh, Mr. Bill or whatever yo name is, I don't 'ppreciate you coming round hea tellin' everbody 'bout my bidness. If I want a real-estater, I'll get me a real estater!"

Needless to say, that lead never became a sale.

Another, perhaps safer, option for obtaining leads is the open house. I'm sure you've been to some. They're usually cool and breezy with refreshments and smiling well-dressed agents. They may ask you to sign in on a sheet or in a little book. Once you do, you're a new lead, someone for them to follow up on over the next few days. They know you came in because you're interested in real estate in some way. Either you're looking to buy or sell or even rent. They don't expect to sell you that particular house. They're looking to help you with something else.

Rarely does an open house sell that day to someone who comes walking in. It's not even the expectation. It's the ultimate hope, but not likely.

The more realistic hope is that some nice lady from down the street will drop by and proclaim she's looking to sell her home. Or that a young couple will stop in and view the property and say it's not for them but they're looking for something else and don't have an agent yet. I myself have never sold a property I was holding open on that very day. Like I said, it rarely happens. Instead I've met people who became future clients with other homes. The nice couple who had the problem with my girlfriend and me living together, yeah, I met them at an open house.

Where I live and work, open houses seem to work best on a weekend, in the afternoon, in spring or fall. Summers are too hot, and God forbid you choose a house where the air conditioning isn't working. No one will want to stay, and neither will you. The same with winter. I've stood trembling, freezing, in houses with no heat in January. I might've had more luck cold-calling on those days!

If I finish up an open house with at least three or four good leads that I believe will become something, I feel I've had a good day. I've had twenty visitors and come away with less. I've had zero visitors and come away with...exactly, zero. You can't always predict it. Nice weather and a busy intersection nearby are usually good things -- until some punk kid comes along and knocks all your signs down. Then you realize why no one came.

Door-knocking and open houses work best for actually meeting potential leads. Though the pivotal face-to-face contact isn't there, you can meet people over the phone. This truly sometimes works or no one would do it. It's worked a few times for me. You just have to say the right stuff and keep them on the line. There are scripts you can study so you're ready for almost any comeback or objection a potential buyer or seller will throw at you. (Just be careful with scripts, or you'll end up sounding robotic, over-rehearsed, and ingenuine.)

Other lead-generating methods are more impersonal, such as direct mail or advertising in newspapers or magazines. You'll have to get pretty good printing and/or mailing rates for these options to be worth your time. An agent told me a few months ago he sent out 9000 mailers and got one listing. Most agents today advertise through some form of social media, be it personal or real estate websites or blogs or whatever they may dream up, because people are creative. You can even buy leads from some sites, though be careful with this. You could be throwing your money away on blanks and duds.

The point is, there are countless ways to find leads (that list I mentioned had sixty). And yes, most leads will be bad and go nowhere. People will tell you what they think you want to hear just to get away from you. Don't be shocked or offended by all the wrong phone numbers and fake emails you'll get. There will be good ones too. Occasionally you'll get the ready-made gift that can close in a week. Sometimes they'll take years to bear fruit. Whatever the case, you'll just need to keep them coming in any way you can, if you want to continue to live the lifestyle.

My favorite door-knocking story involves a house that had a hand-written sign taped over the doorbell:

"DOORBELL IS BROKEN. PLEASE YELL 'DING-DONG' AS LOUD AS YOU CAN."

I left a card on the door but never got a reply. Maybe the door was broken too.

2. TIME IS MONEY

REAL ESTATE UNIT #5387691

I hadn't realized that any of the big real estate companies would readily hire me. There wasn't anything special about me. There isn't anything special about any new agent. They just want numbers. Armies. The more agents, the better. Because the more agents, the more potential money.

New agents are like fresh meat for lions. It's like starting any other "job": you follow directions and do what those around you tell you, since you don't know any better. Everyone seems to be a magic source of knowledge. They all know more than you do. You're a stranger there. That's certainly how I felt on my first day, all spiffy in my new suit and tie. A welcomed stranger. The world spinning around me.

Sign this, sign that, listen to this guy over here give a talk.

Try to understand the convoluted commission structure they blew past you earlier.

How do I get paid?

He's a team leader too?

I thought that lady was a team leader.

Do we all get paid when I sell a house?

The company gets how much?

As they say, it was all a blur. The first week of training went fast. I remember getting to the end of that week, not having made a penny in five days of "work" and yet just being so happy I'd escaped the grimy grind of retail. It had been my happiest work week ever.

I went in blind. Unless you know another agent or two, you just don't have any idea how it works. I didn't know that my mentor would make some extra cash by bringing me into the fold. And I didn't know that the company who wooed me so with their fancy dinner and lipstick would suck up so much of their agents' money.

There it is again.

Money.

They tell you from the first day.

"You're here to make money."

How much money?

As much as you possibly can! That's what it's all about. The cash is out there to grab. Every house with a sale sign in the front yard has a potential check attached to it. Every prospective seller, every inquiring buyer, they're all walking paychecks. Go out there and get it. The cash. It's yours. Take it. Are you gonna let someone else take it? No! Grab it!

You have to be careful not to let them turn you into a money-obsessed zombie.

The more you make, the more they make.

Up to a certain dollar point, that is. Reach it and you're paid off for the year. Then when the new year starts, your cash clock starts again. It's kind of like a "lunch money" concept. When you've surrendered enough of it, you get to keep the rest.

Not all real estate companies operate this way.

Mine did.

To this day they're huge, successful, and still growing, so they must be doing something right.

But wouldn't it have been helpful to me, knowing this before I even joined? And knowing I could've joined any company out there? That I had a choice? That I could've shopped them? Just as new clients shop agents, new agents can shop real estate firms. Nobody told me that.

A wide public perception is that agents make a ton of money. Some do. Most do not. The average is $48,000 a year. Retail store managers surpass that total.

Another thing you may not know is that you do need some cash in the beginning. Those startup fees pile up. On the way to becoming a licensed real estate agent, you can expect to spend $1000 or more on course materials, exams, finger prints, membership fees, and various other things. Once you're licensed, other expenses arise, and keep arising, depending on how you're running your business.

And don't confuse the term Realtor® with "real estate agent". They're two different things.

A Realtor® is a member of NAR, the National Association of Realtors®. A plain old real estate agent is an agent who is not a member.

Don't try to pass yourself as a member of NAR if you're not. You can get fined for things like that.

The yearly NAR membership these days is around $120. Locally you'll also have an association to join. Mine is the Greater Las Vegas Association of Realtors®, or GLVAR. This membership will provide you with tools, training, MLS (Multiple Listing Service) access, and political representation.

Nothing says you have to join these fraternities, but most agents do. You may find yourself at a disadvantage if you don't, especially if you can't use the MLS to serve your clients.

My mentor told me early on, "This job, it costs."

He was right. Good thing I'd gotten into a field where it's all about the money, all the time.

THE TRUTH OF THE MATTER

Commission.

That dirty little word keeps coming up.

Realize, it's all you get. To be a full-time agent, you must be willing to accept that you're not being paid by the hour or supplied a weekly salary. The real estate company you sign on with is not your employer. You are your employer. Your own boss. You may work on a team and be guided or led by a team leader, but even this person is not your boss.

(If you don't do what they ask or suggest, they may just start ignoring you, since you're not helping them make money.)

Your commission, your lone income, is up to you. It can be as high or low as you cause it to be.

Obviously you must close a transaction to receive a commission. You won't make any cash just showing homes or driving those foreign-language-speaking people around in your car. That's for cabbies and Uber drivers. You didn't get a license to do that.

Warning: I'm going to talk some numbers now, so stay with me.

You'll see how funny the commission struggle can be.

Commission is negotiable.

There's no standard.

Six percent is often quoted, as in 3% for a listing agent and 3% for a buyer's agent. It's not 6% for both, as I've had some misinformed clients suggest. Don't we all wish.

It's 3% each.

It can be less. A seller may negotiate for a lower rate. A smart and savvy listing agent, as long as he or she can afford it, will settle for less. They expect that the marketing efforts they'll use for the property will generate multiple calls from interested parties, and this will translate into more buyers or even more sellers. A nice, bright, legible for-sale sign installed in the front yard can work wonders all on its own.

Notice I said, "as long as he or she can afford it".

That agent may be working on a team. The team leader, a more established successful agent, will generate or obtain buyer and seller leads and delegate them to members of the team. The member will then meet the lead – the client – and work with them to help them find a home or get their home sold. Or both. When the transaction closes, the team leader and the member agent split the resulting commission 50/50.

If it's 3% on a $250,000 home, that's $7500. So they would each receive $3750, or 1.5%, correct?

Yes -- if the team leader has paid off his yearly lunch money yet with the company. If he hasn't, that aforementioned $7500 can have as much as 30% in fees and royalties shaved off the top. This reduces it to $5250.

So then each agent receives $2625 – on which he or she will have to pay 15% or more in taxes. Now they're at around $2231.

That's .009% commission on a $250,000 sale. Not a lot of money there. And that's on 3% to start with. Start with 2.5% or less, and you can see how tough it gets.

The math is much simpler at companies who charge only a flat fee, such as $500, per transaction.

The agent makes a sale, pays their fee, and gets to keep the rest of their money. If it's a 50/50 split with another agent, so be it; the fee comes off the top and nothing else.

These agents have more leeway when it comes to the 3%. They can afford to work for less if needed. In a tight, competitive market this is important. With pure numbers they can beat out other agents at getting listings or enticing buyers.

A few years ago a top agent in my area decided he would list homes for 1% for clients with small profit margins, such as those climbing out from being "underwater" with their mortgages. He made it possible for them to sell without having to do short sales.

The gimmick caught on.

He flooded the market with advertising, got a buzz going, hauled in the listings, made lots of people happy, and unwittingly turned himself into a Las Vegas real estate icon. Today the 1% deal is still alive, extended to everyone, and listings keep coming, week after week.

A few years ago he was invited to speak to a roomful of agents at one of these "lunch money" firms.

They brought him in to discuss the latest changes in laws pertaining to real estate. This was during the Great Recession, when every other house on the block was getting foreclosed or being short-sold.

While preparing the crowd for the presentation, one of the higher-ups in the office announced to his sea of agents that they weren't going to be discussing commission. And that commission was not to be discussed. And that no one should be bringing up the subject of commission. You might as well have told a classroom of second graders that a puppy handler was coming to visit them with a fresh litter but that they wouldn't be allowed to pet the puppies.

The speaker gave his talk as scheduled and enlightened everyone about the state of the market, the laws affecting it, and what he envisioned for the months ahead.

"Any questions?" he asked.

A hand went up.

"Yeah?"

Loudly, "How do you list homes for 1%? How can you afford to do that?"

You can just see the office brokers burying their faces in their hands.

Most of those agents there had no idea what the real estate world was like outside their own office, what other options they had. Maybe no one had ever told them. They weren't going to hear it there.

It's all about the money, for sure. You're there to make money.

But whose money is it that you're really making?

HOW MUCH YOU GOT?

If the money isn't there, nothing will happen.

Cash as always is solid. Proof of funds and you're in.

Most buyers today use some kind of financing, which opens up a whole realm of potential problems that can prevent the money from being "there".

When it comes to money, people do get weird. Understand, it's a private matter. Your income, your savings, your taxes, your financial whatever, usually you don't want to give out that information to anyone.

Not that an agent or a lender is just anyone. They're licensed professionals who work every day to make their clients' dreams come true.

Or at least try to.

You've heard of mattress money. That one comes up every once in a while. Some clients don't like to hear that they actually need to have their cash verifiable and available in a financial institution such as a bank or credit union. A mattress is not a bank. Neither is a canvas bag. Nor is a safe under your house.

How can I sell them a property without proof that they have what they say they have? Especially if I barely know them?

A listing agent or seller will be wary of their supposed "cash" offer. On the financing side, no lender will be able to complete their loan.

House-buying and paranoia don't go well together. If you're adverse to sharing necessary info with the appropriate parties, or depositing your money somewhere it can be verified, you should probably steer clear of real estate transactions.

Dealing with money can turn the nicest people into mouth-foaming monsters. New agents beware.

I was working with a couple who wanted to list their previous residence. I'd just helped them through a long nasty short sale and they were thrilled with their new home. And, it seemed, thrilled with me. These were two of the most pleasant, easy-going people you'd ever meet. Vigilant about their money, for sure, but not off the charts about it. And more so the husband than the wife.

They'd made some attractive improvements in the old house and got it ready for market. They asked me to come see it so we could discuss pricing. When I arrived they welcomed me warmly, as always.

The place looked great. I had a list of sold "comps" -- similar homes that have recently sold in the area -- but this house looked better than any of them. I figured that as long as we kept the list price within reason, we could do better than the comps and get the sellers even more money. I explained this to them.

She went berserk. And not a good berserk. I think she even shocked her husband. In her eyes the house was worth much much more than I'd proposed.

I didn't get the listing. They gave it to another agent who listed it for the same price I recommended. Then when it sold, the appraised value came in even lower and they ended up having to sell for less. How glad was I not to be on the receiving end of that!

Now I'm not surprised by people and their "money sides", as I call it.

There was a buyer I called "Mr. 5000".

Really nice guy, mid-fifties, pretty laid-back except when it came to finances. Three times, on three different houses, with three different listing agents and sellers, I had him in a counter offer process. Each time, after his customary low-ball initial offer, it came down to $5000 separating himself and the seller.

On nearly half-million-dollar properties.

He stuck to his principles. He never relented.

I know what he was waiting for. He wanted me to say, "Look, let me put in $2500 of my commission and I'll see if the other agent will do the same. Then we'll have the $5000 you need and we can move forward with the deal."

No way, not for that guy. There's a well-known saying about using other people's money to get rich. Agents need to watch out for those kinds of clients. Mr. 5000 had the money, I know he did. He also knew I had a commission coming and that since agents make so much money....

You get it.

No long ago I had some buyers purchasing a property and selling another. The timeline was tight and we needed to close by the end of the month. The seller for the house they were buying waited till the eleventh hour to order the HOA demand, which is required to close. This simple breakdown of fees can take up to ten days to arrive. Unless you put a rush on it. Then it's 24-48 hours. The rush is $100 extra. Sound like bribery?

The seller refused to pay the $100, so the other agent and I agreed to throw in fifty bucks each in order to meet our timeline. Then a repair that was agreed upon by the seller, that was supposed to have already been taken care of, turned up. We got a bid on it. $400.

Again the seller wouldn't budge. He told his agent, "You and the other agent pay for it. I'm not."

Oh, and he was coming out with over $150K on the sale. Didn't he just want to get this wrapped up so he could receive his big fat check?

Other people's money.

The listing agent did his job and convinced the seller to credit the buyers the $400 from his proceeds at closing so they could get the repair done themselves. We ended up closing a day early.

I can't say I haven't contributed in a few cases where the extra cash was desperately needed. You can sense if it's the right thing to do, the right person/persons to help. You really know it's right when the other agent agrees to work with you on it and help out as well. If you can afford it, there's nothing wrong with that.

The Mr. 5000 case was different. Our last encounter ended up with him getting so fired up and defensive over his personal finances that I sensed he was about to take a swing at me. I suspected he was drunk. At 11 AM.

I learned from his lender that he'd burned through at least four agents in the Las Vegas area over the past few years, so I guess I was number five.

I deleted him from my database after that drunken day, and I don't believe he ever got a house here. He really missed out on those fabulous Recession prices, all over a measly five grand.

I had no choice but to laugh it out with my team. So much misspent energy, so much wasted time. I had to step away – maybe for my own safety!

Even when the money is "there", sometimes things don't happen. People lose their minds over money, and lose other things too, including their real estate agents.

HASTE NOT WASTE

I can't emphasize this enough: as an agent, your time is very important. Since you aren't being paid by the hour, you've got to make the best use of what time you have. This is why you need to be certain you're working with ready, willing, and able buyers as well as motivated sellers. You will quickly learn to discern who's real and who's full of it (and I don't mean full of motivation). Then you can pick and choose who to work with.

Just as clients can "fire" you, you can "fire" clients.

Your job is to make a sale. If that can't happen, why are you there?

There's nothing existential about that. It's very clear.

You hire a plumber to unclog your sink. He has to perform. But you also have to let him in the door when he shows up so he can do his job. A client needs to listen to his or her agent. Otherwise why use one?

Due to one reason or another, we all want things we can't obtain. Buyers and sellers are no different.

You've probably seen the TV shows – whether real or not – where an agent is showing properties to a couple who can't seem to agree on what they want. They have a clearly stated budget, and this budget determines which area of town and which housing features they can afford.

Yet still they complain they're not seeing what they really want. One may desire a swimming pool, while the other wishes to be closer to work. It's up to the agent to find them a property that satisfies them both and also fits within their budgetary restraint.

On TV, they look at maybe three homes, reach a compromise, and purchase something that meets them in the middle somewhere, all the while not costing them more than they can afford.

This is pretty much a fantasy. It's not impossible, but not likely either.

New agents can't be expecting it to go this way.

I had an instructor a few years back in a continuing education class (yes, you'll need to keep going to school periodically to maintain your license) who professed a similar, unthinkable method.

He claimed he'd show buyers up to three homes of the buyers' choosing and then make them decide on one to buy. If they balked at that and asked to see more, he'd tell them to have a nice day and that would be it. He'd drop them as clients.

I don't know any other agents who go by that rule. Maybe it worked for him, I don't know. Maybe he'd found some bottomless font of easily disposable buyer leads.

I do know that good leads are hard to come by, and I know if I treated my clients like that, I wouldn't have any clients.

The truth is that people argue. Couples fight. They need choices. When they don't get them, they can become discouraged. This can eventually lead to giving up.

"We decided we'll just stay where we are."

No agent wants to hear that.

No one, neither couples nor singles, wants homebuying to be difficult. The process itself is not, it's actually quite easy. Locating the property is often the hardest part, especially when inventory is low in a given city or region.

When clients can't find the home they want within their price range, their excitement starts to wane. They start dragging their feet, looking at homes just to look, hoping for something magical to happen. They're still ready and able, but perhaps not as willing anymore. They've realized they may have to "settle" and they're not happy about it. They may even start to believe it's their agent's fault.

Meanwhile the agent is thinking, "Oh crap, what can I do? There's nothing out there for them! I don't want to lose them, I've put so much time into this...."

Some agents today are creating inventory by rehabbing and flipping homes purchased at auction. Fabulous idea, but it may not work for the weary buyer you have right in front of you.

Non-rehabbed auction properties and for-sale-by-owners (FSBO's) in your buyer's preferred area are options, as are any listings you can find through advertising mailers, open houses, door-knocking, cold-calling, internet leads, etc. Some solution must be found or the buyer could disappear, leaving the agent with nothing to show for his or her efforts. It happens.

Says the agent's internal voice:

"You're down. Pick yourself up off the mat. There are other clients."

If that voice can't mutter those words, I'd suggest you try another industry, maybe one that pays you for all your precious minutes and hours.

At least this couple who had so much trouble facing their financial limitations are innocent, nonintentional time-users. I would never call them time-wasters. They wanted the process to be quick and easy, like on TV. They didn't foresee being unable to locate the right home. After all, there are millions of properties available nationwide, right?

Yes. *Nationwide*. Not in one town.

They differ from those who pose as buyers but really have no intention of actually purchasing anything.

These are the most maddening to agents.

The main sign is they never make offers. If someone is making offers and they keep losing out, you know at least they're trying. But when there's no sign of offers and the requests for appointments just keep coming with no progress...red flag. You're no longer an agent. You're a tour guide. Or worse than that, maybe an unpaid taxi driver. You have to cut it off.

Time-suckers have no respect for your time or effort. Which translates to no respect for you and your profession. You're working for them, sure. They gave you a preapproval letter from a lender, sure. And oh man, they're looking at $750K homes, so...you don't want to upset that applecart. Trouble is, you won't be able to afford any apples without income.

You need to sit this client down and have a talk. Chances are, you're not the first agent they've done this to. Some people run through multiple agents and still come up empty-handed. Each agent tried. Each failed. There will likely be another after you. So why continue if there's no promise of a sale? Some folks can't make decisions. They can't commit. Why should you become a victim of that?

Get out.

Fire them.

Mr. 5000, anyone?

Again, real estate is about relationships. Some are great, some are dysfunctional. You probably already have enough dysfunction in your family. You don't need it at work too, if you can help it.

And in this job -- this *lifestyle* -- you can.

I just heard an agent last week declare he would no longer work with buyers under a certain price-point because it was just getting too hard to find them deals. That's his choice, he can do that. I wouldn't recommend it. In this business, things have a way of coming back around to get you, like a weird form of karma. I say, don't prejudge or stereotype those little difficult deals. Those folks could turn out to be the greatest buyers and sellers, the greatest clients, you'll ever have.

CHECK THE SCHEDULE

You have to be capable of managing your time.

You may have gobs of it or none. With no daily clock to punch, your life can easily turn into either a chaotic mess or a complacent slumber-fest.

Real estate has seasons: summer being the best, winter the worst.

Traditionally, when school gets out in June, families relocate. Sellers list since they know the market will be hot. As an agent you may be lucky enough to get yourself some "two-fers", someone both buying and selling. If you get several of these stacked up at the same time, along with any other deals you may already be working on, and you're handling all the paperwork and clients yourself, you'll be pretty busy.

You'll be running at high speed, envisioning big dollar signs. You're living the agent's life.

No ceiling.

Day or night, you're always on. Open for business. The phone rings at dinner time. Another referral? Terrific! When can we meet? Tonight after dinner? Perfect, see you then!

It doesn't have to be that crazy. People who aren't agents believe we have no time for ourselves or family and that we're constantly working, never resting. (Funny, are these the same people who complain about how lazy we are and that we never do any work?)

It's true, we work a lot. Since it's not a 9 to 5 job, our hours vary. Our days vary too. When you're starting out, coaches will preach that you need to set a regular weekly schedule for yourself. This can be done. You can set it and follow it – as long as you can deviate from it if needed.

Priorities matter.

Say I've arranged to door-knock a neighborhood between 3 and 5 PM on Thursday. On Wednesday a lady calls me off one of my signs and says she's moving her mother out of her house and needs to list the property ASAP. She'll be at the house tomorrow at 4 PM and can I meet her there?

"I'm sorry," I reply, "I can't, I'll be door-knocking at that time."

No. I'm there. Screw the door-knocking. Why am I doing that anyway? To find sellers!

Most coaches or team-leads won't have a problem with this. If you get one who does, lose them fast.

If that lady had requested to meet me off my schedule, such as later in the evening, I would've had to see what was going on in my life. I won't cancel a preplanned event with my eight-year-old daughter to go visit with that seller lead instead.

I'd explain, "Actually I'm already booked for tonight. Would it be possible to meet sometime tomorrow?"

Most people are reasonable. We all have lives. If she can agree to that, then perfect. We'll meet the next day. If she can't, maybe that's a warning sign. Don't work with people who disrespect you and your time. Let her call someone else.

Then there's the buyer who needs to see a property NOW.

At 8 PM.

Again, consideration must be taken.

You worked all day and now you're on the couch with your significant other or your kids watching TV, and Jane the buyer wants your help. This wasn't part of that weekly schedule you drew up.

How qualified is she? How long have you been working with her? How far away is the property from your place?

If Jane's been beat out repeatedly on offers and can't find anything, and she just came upon a brand new listing you know would work for her, well, maybe it's worth the trip. Make sure you can see the house that late and then invite the wife or hubby or kids or whomever to come along for an evening drive.

This rarely ever happens. I think I've done it twice. Both times they were excellent clients who gave me lots of business. They knew me, I knew them. I made an exception for them and they were most gracious.

It's different when that call comes from someone new.

Are they preapproved to buy? Are they really serious? Do they live locally or just visiting? Are they axe murderers?

You don't want to start out taking orders over the phone from people you don't know. That's when you pull the schedule card.

"Could we meet there tomorrow between 12 and 2? Or maybe Wednesday after 2 PM?"

Give them a choice. See how they react. You're already showing them you're a professional with duties and appointments sprinkled throughout your week. If they can negotiate a day and time with you, great. They'll probably also be happy to bring along or send you their preapproval letter or proof of funds to purchase a home.

If they won't relent and still demand to see the house that night, you know what you should do. Push back. Otherwise you'll be walking around with shoe marks across your back.

It's highly important to stay in control of your time, especially when you're really busy. You won't be available all the time, so don't let clients feel they can simply call you anytime and you'll jump. We all have to make appointments to see doctors and attorneys and other professionals. Why should you run your business any differently? Are you desperate for deals? Sometimes you might be. Don't let them sense that. Keep to the schedule.

Winter can get dark and cold. For agents it can get pretty dreary too. Unless you've kept your lead pipeline full of eager buyers and sellers, you might find yourself filling time decorating a tree or sipping eggnog while watching movies, since there won't be much else to do.

I don't know about you, but going a month or two without eating or paying the mortgage isn't an option I'd want to face.

The truth is, people tend to hunker down during the holidays and forget about real estate for a while. Who wants to move during Christmas? And who wants strangers tracking snow and mud through their homes?

There are buyers and sellers in December, of course, just fewer of them.

As the holidays approach, I remind my buyers that winter is the best time to buy. There's less competition. Not like the summer, when every other house has multiple offers. December and January are full of good deals. Hearing this, they may wait till then to jump into the market. Others who've been in hiding throughout the summer and fall may re-emerge.

I tell my sellers they'll see less competition as well, with fewer homes on the market. This can generate more showings, which translate into offers.

It's the truth. Sure, it could be seen as spin, but it's still true.

MAYBE WE CAN'T AFFORD THAT NOW....

Cancellations happen.

Oh, they can hurt.

Imagine you're about to close escrow on a $750,000 home for your buyer. Or buyers. Everyone is excited and all is going well. Your payday on that could be in the neighborhood of $20,000. In your head you're already dividing up the cash. You and the listing agent are texting with giddy emojis. How awesome is this! An atmosphere of total joy and cooperation. Everyone working toward the same prosperous, fulfilling goal. It happens all the time. Big houses close every day. Now you're gonna get a piece of the pie!

It's four days till closing and suddenly your client gets quiet.

Quiet is bad.

Just like in relationships, communication is Number One in real estate transactions. When things go silent, especially abruptly, it's just a bad sign.

Now the buyer's lender won't respond to your phone calls or emails.

What the heck is going on?

The listing agent, who's ready to get this thing wrapped, is bugging you for answers. Did the buyer(s) sign their papers yet? Did you do a final walk-through on the property? You coolly let them know you're working on it.

Coolly, I say, on the outside. Inside you're panicking.

Then comes the call from the lender. The buyer was let go from his job. The loan is kaput. So is the deal.

You call the client to find out what happened. They let it go to voicemail because they're embarrassed or ashamed or devastated.

There will be no signing, no final walk-through.

Probably no more emojis either.

It's your job to deliver the news to the listing agent, who then has to relay it to his or her seller, who's already scheduled a moving truck to bring their entire household of belongings to the brand new home waiting for them – the brand new home still owned by the builder, who's been very patient and is now starting to apply pressure to get the house closed and off their books.

Ouch.

Everyone will be upset. It's not your fault. You did your job. You did all things necessary to get here. It's not your buyer's fault either. They also did everything right. Maybe they did something wrong at work, who knows? At least, as far as this transaction was involved, they sparkled. Got all their documents to the lender on time, cooperated throughout the inspection period, showed up for all appointments, communicated flawlessly.

The seller too, and their agent: they were great. Accepted your client's offer with very little counter or trouble, worked with your crazy schedules, kept you updated on the progress of repairs, stayed professional and even-tempered. It's all you could ask for. Apparently the buyer and the seller had even become chummy and traded recipes during a cookie break on the back patio.

This is a disaster, this news of cancellation. Sure, it's not your fault, but you, the buyer's agent, you have to take the hit.

The bullet.

Phone calls like this are horrible to make. You try an email instead, just to get the word out. But even then, there will still be a phone conversation. There may be shouting and finger-pointing. I've had listing agents disgustedly hang up on me.

You've just made their job incredibly difficult. They just went from smooth waters to a hurricane in a matter of seconds. You could be that listing agent. Imagine being her, having to notify her seller that the deal has fallen apart due to buyer financing and that the house has to go back on the market.

It's not just a loss of money or a matter of inconvenience, it's a wounding of confidence. The seller hired that agent to sell their home. Now it looks like she can't get the job done. Or that she recommended the seller take a risky offer. In the eyes of the seller, it now becomes the listing agent's fault.

In short it's a big mess.

And that $20K commission you'd already figuratively deposited in your bank account? Gone. Along with the buyer, who now can't qualify to buy an outhouse.

Sometimes things go south for others reasons. I had a buyer who was supposed to pay off a property while attempting to buy another. This was a stipulation of the loan, between the buyer and the lender. Three days before closing I hear from the lender. The buyer didn't perform. Never paid off the other house. First I'd heard of that! So the loan couldn't happen. Dead deal. The listing agent reamed me. Clearly the buyer's own fault.

I learned a few months later he was divorcing his wife.

See the kinds of things we can get caught up in?

A bad inspection can ruin your deal too. Something unexpected turns up and the buyer freaks out. Here you can really see what your buyer is made of. Do they truly like the house? Are they as motivated as they seem? Will repairs or seller credits help pacify them?

As their agent, this is your chance to make it good again any way you can.

Most items you can fix or get fixed. But a broken or cracked foundation, for example, that's usually a killer. One of my buyer's properties had an old leaking pool. No one could tell where it was leaking from. Extensive work would be required and the seller wasn't going to pay for it.

The buyer walked.

Although cancellations like this are disappointing, they don't surprise anyone. They come early in the process. There's no bomb dropped at the last moment. There's a path forward. Find another house, make another offer.

Again, pick yourself up. The world's not ending. You still have your ready, willing, and able buyer.

The same goes for bad appraisals.

Say you're selling a property and an acceptable offer comes in from a buyer who'll be using financing. Great, nothing wrong with that. But remember that the buyer's loan will be subject to an appraisal from the lender. You'll need to prepare your seller for that.

What if the appraisal comes in lower than the agreed-upon purchase price? It can and does happen. Will your seller be willing to drop their price to the appraisal figure or meet the buyer somewhere in the middle?

The lender will only lend up to the appraised value. Anything above that, the buyer has to come out of pocket to cover.

In normal, balanced markets, most buyers will balk at paying above appraisal because this means they're paying more than the house is estimated to be worth and can be insured for. These days, after the pain of the Great Recession, that's a major concern.

Quite a few buyers today using financing don't have the extra cash to make up the difference anyway. And your seller may be stuck on his price. If these two issues converge, you have a problem. If a new purchase price can't be negotiated somehow, the deal will die and the property will have to go back on the market. Yet what happens more often is that the seller, already emotionally separated from the house and eager to get settled in his new place, throws his hands up and accepts the appraised value. He may not be happy with you (as if it's your fault) but at least he's not cancelling the sale.

Just don't give in to the desire to supply him with the appraiser's home address.

Cancellations.

I knew an agent who was trying to complete a short sale for a client in horrible health. Over several months the poor old guy kept going in and out of the hospital, and they literally had him signing papers from the bank in his hospital bed. The agent was worried because if the seller died, the short sale would be canceled. The house wouldn't close and he wouldn't get paid.

I don't know if that's an illustration of a greedy agent or an example of how short sales take too long. Well, the client expired and everything fell apart. The house went back to the bank in foreclosure. I know that one really stung, and I wasn't even involved.

OPEN FOR BUSINESS

You have to be flexible.

And I'm not talking about yoga.

You have to be able to adjust. Just because you learn how to do something one way, doesn't mean there aren't other ways too.

As an agent you'll likely face something called "shift". Basically that's when a certain new dimension is introduced into a housing market, causing a change of direction.

The bursting of the housing bubble during the 2008 financial crisis is an extreme example.

What was once a solid sellers' market morphed overnight into a free-for-all buyers' market. If you owned a home at that time, you know what happened to your value, and how quickly it happened.

Prices plummeted. Owners couldn't sell because they couldn't price their homes low enough. They had to keep chasing the market downward. Many gave up. This resulted in a nationwide barrage of foreclosures. For those who still wanted to sell and avoid foreclosure, a new phenomenon emerged, the short sale, which required homeowners to get approval from their mortgage companies, or "banks", to sell for less than the property was worth.

If you were an agent during this financial hurricane, especially in a hard-hit spot like Las Vegas, you had to learn new stuff and fast.

Regular, traditional sales between buyer and seller had become the minority, replaced by cold, long-drawn-out transactions between buyer and bank, with the selling and listing agents as intermediaries.

To survive, agents had to take crash courses in how to deal with banks and navigate short sales. If they resisted, they could go out of business. A great many did.

It was a new norm, a major shift, requiring a career-saving adjustment.

It took a few years, but the market got past that. What came next was another case of shift.

As things gradually returned to normal, prices began to rise again – in some areas, too quickly.

We started to see a problem with home appraisals. Remember I mentioned that earlier?

You're a buyer's agent and your client falls hard for a certain property. You submit an offer and work to get it accepted, and everyone's happy. You and your buyer feel pretty good about the price of the house. Personally you feel it's a tad high but that the extra upgrades the seller has added justify the higher price. Plus the lot is pretty big, larger than most others in the neighborhood, so it seems there shouldn't be a problem.

Your buyer's lender orders an appraisal and two weeks later it comes back.

$20,000 below the agreed-upon purchase price.

You gasp. How can that be? Surely something was missed. There's a mistake. The buyer is freaking out.

You contact the lender, who then contacts the appraiser, who then refuses to revisit the situation and his valuation of the property. He feels he's used the correct data available to him, going back up to six months, and that the purchase price, based on that data, isn't justified. The buyer doesn't have an extra $20,000 to throw into the pot. Will the seller come down in price? Will the buyer lose the house?

Back then, there was a bunch of that going on as the old market tried to catch up with the new one. It took at least six months to get balanced again. That's a lot of broken deals and damaged relationships.

When hundreds, or thousands, or millions, of agents discover they're having the same difficulty or seeing the same pattern, and it becomes their collective main problem, that's how they know they're in the midst of a shift.

Either they deal with it by sharpening their skills and better educating their clients, or they take the resulting body blows that can harm or destroy their livelihood.

Too much inventory, not enough inventory, prices too high, prices not low enough, even emerging technologies – all are causes of shift. Though each housing market is different, they can share the same issues. This goes for agents as well.

A good strong agent will react to change. Maybe it's their marketing technique. Maybe it's the services they offer. Someone will always try to be a step ahead of you. It's no different than the retail industry, where established companies fold all the time due to an inability to capture enough business.

During the hard days of the housing bust, millions of agents "hung up", or suspended, their licenses. They couldn't make any money, they couldn't compete. Either they just didn't want to put in the effort or perhaps they just weren't meant to be agents in the first place.

I've heard it said that back in 2006, you only had to be breathing to make $100K in a year as a real estate agent in Las Vegas. If you weren't making that kind of cash, there had to be something wrong with you. Everyone was buying, everyone was selling, loans were easy to get. High prices, high commissions, it was boomtime, one of those eras when it was fashionable to be an agent. Outside technology such as real-estate-related websites and apps hadn't totally usurped the client yet. Agents still had control. The multiple listing service was King. No one had any idea what was coming!

Post-bust, as the market started its long steady recovery – a monolithic shift in itself – real estate gained popularity again. Old agents trickled back into the game. Newbies got themselves tested and licensed. It was stylish again to boast you had a real estate license so you could make your friends think you had an awesome flow of income, despite the fact that you only did it part-time while maintaining your safe bi-weekly wage at the salon or the post office.

Inevitably, time will test these agents again. A coming tsunami, seen from the great beach of real estate, will challenge them to make moves, change course.

I can still see what one of my early coaches wrote on the white board one day before a presentation:

"Shift happens."

WHAT WAS THAT ABOUT A PAPERLESS SOCIETY?

Do you like paperwork?

Are you an organized person?

You'll be amazed at how many trees the real estate industry kills.

If you've ever sold or purchased a home, you'll remember the stack of paperwork you had to initial and sign just before closing. Escrow officers and their assistants get lots of papercuts. You'll get them too as you drop sheet after sheet into your manila or hanging folders. This is a good thing. You'll *want* to be dropping lots of sheets into lots of folders.

If you can't deal with paperwork, you could always hire an assistant, but this person will need to be paid in more than papercuts, so you'll need to be doing some good business.

Most agents use what we call a Transaction Coordinator. Mine is fantastic. I send her all my buyer or seller docs, and she molds them into a complete electronic file for my broker, covering all the bases so that once a property closes I can get paid in a timely manner (usually within 1-2 days if no required docs are missing). Her nominal fee is totally worth it.

In the meantime, however, someone has to get all that paperwork collected to send to her. That would be me.

She could do it for me, sure, but since she's usually working on 75 to 100 escrows at a time, I prefer to do that part on my own.

I don't mind paperwork. In fact I'm probably a bit OCD about it. And as an agent, if there's anything you'd really want to be OCD about, it's your files.

If they aren't complete, you won't get paid.

Your office will give you a list of required items. They all have to be there. The reason for this is based in law. Or fear of lawsuits, I should say.

In case a buyer or seller chooses to sue for whatever reason after closing on a home, a full and thorough file will help protect you and your broker. It's that simple. Your broker will hold your commission check hostage until you come up with that one last missing piece of paper, signed by both buyer and seller.

Sometimes these pieces of paper are hard to come by after closing if you failed to obtain them during the escrow process, so be diligent.

Don't be sloppy. Use one folder for each file. Check your list and make sure you get everything. Or make sure your assistant or whoever does.

It would be embarrassing to be splitting a deal with another agent, and at the end, that agent can't pick up their check because everyone's waiting on you to come up with some buyer disclosures you should've had three weeks before.

A scattered agent is an unsuccessful agent.

One thing your assistant or transaction coordinator can't do for you is *read* paperwork.

We all roll our eyes at the long legal agreements that pop up whenever we want to buy a product or service online.

"Who actually reads that stuff?" people complain.

Well, somebody does.

Probably attorneys, and people who've been screwed before in some way or another.

The truth is, we all should read them. They're there for a reason (usually to protect the person or company selling the product or providing the service).

My fourth grade teacher had a talent for reading upside down. From a good distance too. She amazed us every day with that skill. This is something you may want to practice – unless you can get familiar enough with your local paperwork that you already know what it says when a buyer or seller questions you about it.

The residential purchase agreement we currently use for buyers in Southern Nevada is 10 pages long. It's written in fairly straightforward English so that most people can read and understand it. If they have questions, I explain further. I know it well enough so that I don't have to read it upside down if I happen to be with them when they're going through it.

Taking it from them and silently reading a section to yourself in front of them makes you look ~~like a buffoon~~ like you're unfamiliar with the document, which may cause them to lose confidence in you as their representative in the transaction. It happened to me in my early days. I didn't like how it felt.

Same with the 8-page listing agreement. You have to know what all those paragraphs and clauses mean. You have to read them and be able to explain them. You can't wing it. Just because we're in a technological age when many of these agreements are signed electronically and we don't always have to be sitting there with the client and a pen, doesn't mean we can be lazy and not really know what we've sent them to sign.

There are normal things we see in almost every contract. Buyers usually pay for certain things, as do sellers. You come to expect paperwork to be written that way.

A "clean" offer on a property will have all the points touched upon in the generally accepted manner with no mistakes or anomalies. Which basically means it has a much better chance of being accepted.

One time I saw a ludicrously lowball offer that also asked for all the furniture. The seller gasped.

"Do they want my firstborn too?"

Newbie paperwork can be glaringly bad. It's best for a new agent to have a team leader or a more experienced agent review his stuff before he sends it to the listing agent. You don't want your money miscalculations, missed checkmarks, blank lines, and wild requests to spoil your offer.

Remember, your client is counting on you to deliver their message in a professional way. Even veteran agents who don't do many deals per year can screw up if they're not careful.

From time to time, the powers-that-be in your local association will revise the standard forms you use. They'll give you notice, but if you're not watching you could miss it. These changes can be something as little as one line to as big as an entire document.

When they revised our residential purchase agreement last year, the changes were so drastic, my broker arranged a breakfast buffet and brought us all together, hundreds of agents, to go over the new contract line by line.

If you were a part-time agent who didn't bother to keep up on these kinds of things, you would've been shocked the next time you had to write up an offer for a buyer.

Where did this clause come from?

Where did that paragraph go?

You don't want to be asking yourself those questions in the heat of trying to beat out other offers on your buyers' newest, most favorite find.

Stay up to date.

I won't even go into when the MLS system gets a complete facelift every 5 years or so. Everybody hates that, since everybody hates change.

The MLS is the main tool for your business. Suddenly it'll have a whole new look with new features. Plus, that search bar that used to be at the top is now at the bottom. That kind of thing. For about a year, everyone knows it's coming. You can't miss it even if you're living under a rock. And for about a year everyone complains that the current system is fine, and why do they have to change it?

Hey, companies all over the world do this all time. Why should this be any different?

We all learn the new platform and get used to it. We move on. It'll happen again, and we'll do it again. And in the end we'll grow to like it. We can't work without it.

Huh, I guess I did go into it. Oh well, that was good for you to hear. Now you know.

Imagine turning on your MLS for the first time in 2 months (as some 85er's do) and seeing a whole new screen and platform that you don't know how to navigate.

Yikes!

Stay up to date.

Your clients will be able to tell if you're not.

And on a side note, while we're talking about legal forms, here's something to keep in mind: you're not an attorney.

Again, you're not attorney.

And if you try to act like one, or give advice like one, you could have big trouble coming your way.

If you've gone to law school and have training in that field, that's different. You have an advantage because you can help your clients in more ways than one. You're much more handy for them to have around. Most agents don't have this extra training or degree.

A smart agent will have a dependable real estate attorney or two in their phone for times when clients' questions or problems inch toward the legal realm. It only makes sense. Why take a chance trying to answer something when you're not really sure what you're talking about, especially if people's lives and money are at stake?

That's a third rail if there ever was one.

We have lots of forms. If something new comes up, we get a new one. They're drafted and approved by lawyers to protect us. The signature of Jim Client states that he understands it and relieves us of potential harm.

Agents are asked to participate in legal activity – the conveying of property – without a law degree. Clearly things could get messy, ugly, fast. That's why we have heavily-insured brokers to manage our offices, and why we have so many forms to use.

That pesky paperwork could end up saving you bigtime. Because after all, you're working with people, and people are the most trying of all creatures.

3. IT'S A PEOPLE BUSINESS

NOT YOUR GRANDPA'S REAL ESTATE AGENT

There was a time, apparently, way back in the twentieth century, when clients actually came to agents looking for properties.

There was also a time when folks known as travel agents booked your flights to Hawaii or Paris for you.

Don't get me wrong, I'm not saying that the real estate agent is going the way of the travel agent. Of course not. Real live human real estate agents will always be needed. But technology has changed things dramatically and will continue to do so.

I remember, as a kid, reading the flyers of the latest listings in the windows of realty offices in San Francisco. The offices were small and dark inside, at least from the outside, with their venetian blinds half-drawn. They seemed full of secret information. Because they were.

You wanted to purchase a home, so you went in to meet with one of the people who worked in there. You discussed with them what you were looking for and how much you could spend. Maybe you'd seen some For Sale signs on lawns in your neighborhood or driving around town. Yet you really had no idea how many homes were on the market. You weren't quite sure what they were going for either, unless you talked to a neighbor or someone who knew what Al down the street got for his place. And even then, how could you know if that was really the truth? Your best source was the newspaper if they published info about local home sales, or maybe the county assessor's office.

You didn't have easy access to all-things-real-estate back then. That's why you had to go chat with your local agent in the little office. He knew everything. He had a "database" of homes that only the agents knew about -- the MLS. It wasn't even on a computer. It was a small printed book that needed to be updated constantly. You discussed which properties would work best for you, then you went to see them.

If you found something you liked and wanted to offer on, you'd go back to the office, or the agent would come to your house, and you'd go over a type-written contract and fill in the blanks by hand. Over time, you know what happened. The MLS became computerized and so did the contracts and forms. Soon clients could sign electronically, remotely, without a pen.

But there was more.

The lone agent with all the secrets in the dark little office was losing control. Information was leaking out. The internet, with all its delights and all its power, had started to capture the attention and imagination of the everyday consumer.

As it grew, more and more stuff, from news to goods to services, could be found there all the time, including real estate. Websites advertising homes for sale began to pop up. Buyers and sellers took notice and basked in this newfound freedom and independence. No longer did they have to crawl to the agent to be shown the way. Now they could find it on their own in the comfort of their home office, or even from their couch or bed. Or toilet.

Today buyers let us know which properties they'd like to see. They find something they like online and ask us about it. Then we go to the MLS, still the ultimate authority (some secrets remain) and let them know if it's available or if there's some dirty laundry they need to know about before considering it.

This dirty laundry, or sensitive agent-to-agent information, is what clients don't get to see on their consumer sites. It may be anything from warnings about aggressive dogs or uncooperative sellers/tenants to bank stipulations/disclosures to private phone numbers or emails. It's up to you, the agent, to handle this info with care. You can get fined by your local Real Estate Division (the RED) if you don't.

It's also up to you to educate a client who thinks they know everything there is to know about a property.

The truth is that technology has not only empowered the real estate consumer but sort of corrupted him as well. The consumer's knowledge is only as good as the information he gets from the websites he visits. Traditionally some of these sites have shown to be outdated and thus misleading.

Clients trust them because they know you can believe everything you read on the internet!

I'm out with them looking at homes. They pull out their phone and go, "I saw this property on blankety-blank.com. Can you see if it's still available? I'd really like to go see it!"

I check the MLS and reply, "Actually that one's under contract. Looks like they're due to close in a week or so."

"But my app says it's for sale."

"It is. But it's not available. Someone else is in the process of purchasing it."

"Huh?"

"Is it on the list of available properties I sent you from the MLS?"

"No."

"Then it's not available."

They're dumbfounded by this. They gaze at their phone as if they've been lied to by their favorite site. I let them know that if it falls out of escrow, it'll come back on the market and then we can view it. (Note: Philosophies differ here. Some agents will still show houses even if they're under contract with another buyer, which usually brings the wrath of the listing agent, who'll tell you you have no business being in there.)

When you can show the client you have some extra, or up to date, info on a property, they see your value as an agent. That is, unless they choose to believe their favorite app and decide you're lying to them. With the abundance of data readily available these days, some people just don't know who or what to believe anymore.

You have to be on your game. Consumer real estate sites are working to get better all the time. There's only so much business out there, and they want to snatch that client away from you. So now not only are you competing with other agents, you're competing with websites that are looking to eliminate you from the market and send you into the big black hole where all the travel agents went.

Online listing services allow sellers to list as a for-sale-by-owner (FSBOs), or they can choose to pay some nominal fees and get representation from an agent on the site. Others go further. Say you'd like to sell your home quickly or don't want dozens of buyers traipsing through the house. These services provide you with the answers to those problems. On their sites, after you provide and submit information about your property, they make you a cash offer that allows you to close whenever you want without any hassle. No buyers, no agents. No people. Just cold hard cash, just the way you like it.

They have solutions for buyers too. Ninety percent of buyers start their search online these days, so why wouldn't these sites want to capture and keep them? With the help of a cyber-agent, or a real agent posing as one, you can pick out a property you like and make your offer without even having to leave home.

In this age of shopping online, and texting or messaging instead of phone calls, this lack of human contact is just fine with the modern consumer, particularly the Millennial. He or she sees no reason to indulge in a shallow pseudo-relationship with another person – an agent - and brave things like weather or traffic in order to do something they can do right from home. The concept of the all-knowing guy with the info book in the little office downtown would seem ludicrous to them, almost like out of an old movie. They don't need him. He's dead. He's yesterday.

So how do you, a live, breathing, capable agent, compete with this mindframe and the technological advances that have perpetuated it? Well, believe it or not, there are still plenty of clients out there who need you. They want someone to trust. They need guidance, hand-holding even.

It's like the battle of big-box retail vs. smaller chains.
When I worked in the drugstore industry, we had higher prices than the big-box competition. This is still the case today. To combat this, the smaller stores boast shorter lines and more personal friendly service, which is usually true. A young mother may decide it's easier to walk across the street to a smaller store for baby formula than to get in the car and drive two or three miles to a bigger place. She'll get in and out quicker, and home quicker. She may pay a little more, but she feels the convenience is worth it.

As an agent with a friendly confident smile, knowledge of the local real estate market, and enough patience to guide your clients through a process completely alien to them, you can beat out cold, faceless, mechanical competitors, especially if you can match or beat their fees. Because people still need people. They need a sounding board.

When buyers complain about too much paperwork, I tell them they're not buying a bunch of bananas, they're buying a house. And they usually chuckle, because a simple comment like that reminds them of the complexity of things and how they can quickly lose touch with what they're trying to do.

Websites won't joke with them or hold their hand.

But you can. The guy in the little office probably did. Don't forget you're his descendent, his successor, keeping his legacy alive, just on a much bigger scale.

DO UNTO OTHERS....

I believe in karma.

I believe the universe has a way of correcting, or righting, itself. Call me superstitious, whatever. I don't think I'm alone.

When I was in high school and had no money, I ducked into a used bookshop one day and found a very early hardbound copy of Freud's *The Interpretation of Dreams*, published around 1920. I was into that kind of stuff at the time and just couldn't pass it up. It cost me twenty bucks, which I hadn't counted on spending on an antique book. This left me with just enough for a cheap early dinner and the bus ride home.

After leaving the shop, I was walking down the street and noticed something small and bunched up on the sidewalk in front of me. I bent down to inspect it.

Money!

I snatched it up and unrolled it.

Not only money. Twenty bucks!

How awesome was that! I'd found a nice literary prize *and* gotten my money back. Sweet.

I stuffed it in my pocket and marched happily on to a burger joint at the corner.

All through the meal I kept my book safely next to me in its plain yellow plastic bag, never taking it out for fear of getting ketchup or something on it.

I waited till I could see the bus coming and rushed out to catch it.

I jumped on and grabbed a pole, packed tight amongst the other riders. More than halfway home – and I'm talking a fifty-minute ride across town – I realized I was missing something.

Yep, I'd left my book in the restaurant.

It was getting late and I didn't know how long it would take to get back over there. Buses could take forever, and I didn't have enough cab money. No cell phone either. I couldn't call till I got home.

I reached the manager and explained my desperate situation. She checked her lobby and her lost-and-found, then came back on the line.

No yellow bag, no Freud.

So now I still had the twenty bucks, but I'd lost what I really wanted. I would've traded the cash for that book.

It was like an invisible force saying, "You weren't supposed to have that book. Now things have been corrected."

I'll never forget that. It's a sort of barometer I use in my life for when things are going extraordinarily well. People who know me will tell you I'm an eternal optimist, which I proudly am...but I'm also cautious.

Here's another reason why.

A few years ago I had a great streak of closings going on with both buyers and sellers. My whole team was killing it. I landed a new listing, right near my house. Wonderful big home with a pool. In June. In Las Vegas. Just perfect.

Within the first week, we received four offers. I helped my sellers select the best of the four and we went into escrow.

Two weeks later I got an email from one of the rejected buyers. He'd seen my contact info on the offer paperwork. He'd secured a new job in Las Vegas and was planning to move here from another state. Fine. Only one problem. He couldn't find a house. He kept getting outbid. He'd reached the point now where he felt it was his agent's fault.

His offer on my listing had been a good one, over list price, just not as good as the one we took. He saw I had a listing and figured I knew what listing agents were looking for at the time. Toward the end of his message, he asked me flat out if I believed I could help him get an offer accepted. Of course I would say yes – even though I knew that by doing so, I was taking someone else's client.

In the email string, I could see his agent's name and photo. I didn't know the guy. I'd never heard of him. And I hadn't solicited his buyer, he'd come to me. Fair game. Happens all the time. Win some, lose some. How many clichés could there be for this? Lots, and I knew it had happened to me, so I went for it. I was hot and knew I could help this guy.

Keep my closing streak alive.

By early August I had him all finished, moving into his new home. This, only one week after closing on the big pool property.

I felt great.

Powerful.

"Who's next?" I called out to the world. "How much more can I do?"

That sounds stupid, right?

Well, that's how I felt – stupid - about six months later after the worst parade of stops and starts and cancellations and bad luck I'd ever experienced in my real estate career. It really seemed like I'd been cursed.

The guy who'd lost his client to me, he couldn't have done that. He didn't know me.

But the universe did.

Perhaps I'd received something I shouldn't have.

This essentially boils down to ethics.

If my old book story doesn't seem to relate to ethics, as you understand it, consider if I'd picked up that twenty note and turned it in to the police, like a lost wallet. That would've been the most honest thing to do. But I didn't. I would guess that most people wouldn't. Is that unethical?

What if I'd contacted that agent and let him know his buyer wanted to drop him and work with me? I *know* the majority of agents would laugh at that idea. Was it ethical to take his client and leave him wondering what had happened?

As things go, that's small stuff compared to what you could face in this industry.

You're taking a new listing and your seller claims the house has a building defect. Something's wrong with the foundation. He even gets a golf ball, sets it on the wooden family room floor, and lets it roll, of its own volition, across the room to the wall.

Wow, you just saw that. There's definitely a tilt.

He'd like to sell, he just doesn't want to disclose to potential buyers that the foundation is probably sinking. Oh, and there were some wall cracks too, but he's puttied them and repainted. No one needs to know.

Business has been slow this winter and you really need this listing.

Yet can you really work with this guy? What else is he hiding? And can you imagine the potential legal troubles if a buyer discovers the problems after closing?

He also mentions he won't sell to minorities.

"I won't do that to my neighbors."

Here you have an ethical firetrap. Unless you can convince him to disclose the tilt issue and consider any offer that may come in, this listing could mean big headaches for you, and costly ones too.

He's not acting ethically, and if you go along with his wishes, you aren't either.

Take a buyer situation where you might be tipped off to something by a home inspector.

Your young buyers, new parents, are super excited about this property. You've been working with them for about a month, consistently touring homes. Their first few offers didn't work out, but now they've got this place and it's inspection time.

You know the inspector; you've worked with him several times. The buyers have placed their confidence in him, since they've done the same with you. The house is thirty years old but in good shape. You don't anticipate too many problems. That is, at least nothing you can't get past. It's being sold as-is, no repairs by the seller. The buyers know that.

Halfway through the process you break away from the buyers to check on the inspector and see how things are coming along.

He's in the yard. Just came down from the old shingle roof.

"Pretty spongy up there," he says.

"Soft spots?"

"All over."

"Any leaks?"

"Not sure yet. Gotta check the attic."

"OK."

Meanwhile you're cautious and a little worried, so you don't say anything to the buyers yet. You know they can't afford a new roof. They barely have enough for the down.

When he's done in the attic, you go see him again.

"Lotta stains," he reports.

It hasn't rained in quite a while, so there's no moisture. But a big storm could bring trouble. Surprisingly there aren't any visible stains on the ceiling inside the house. Did the seller paint over them?

"Man, this'll kill the deal," you tell him.

The inspector studies you a moment.

"The stains are old," he says. "It's not leaking right now. I could just say in the report they'll need to monitor the situation. I can recommend roof repair. Doesn't mean they have to replace the whole thing."

"But they probably should, right?"

He smiles. "I would."

You gaze at the floor. You know what's the right thing to do.

You don't want to risk cancelling this escrow. You don't want to have to start over with the home search. And yet you surely don't want a phone call when the next big rain storm hits and the ceiling of the baby's room is pissing water in three places.

It's your duty to give them the truth. You're representing them. They believe in you. If you fib, or withhold information, you're worthless to them. They may as well be representing themselves, blind as they are about the homebuying process. It's Ethics 101.

So you tell them about the roof. It's soft and leaky and most likely needs to be replaced. This could run six to eight thousand dollars. The seller won't do it. In your mind you know that "as-is" listings usually stay that way. The right buyer will come along for them eventually. Your buyers are troubled. Disappointed. But you won't give up yet. You tell them you'll speak with the listing agent to try and squeeze some mercy out of the seller.

Once you have the inspection report in hand, you make the call. The listing agent is cold. She reminds you it's clearly stated: no seller repairs.

"I realize that," you argue. "What about a buyer credit? Can they do that?"

"Let me check."

Now you wait. The rest of the house checked out surprisingly well. All other recommended repairs can be done over time and by the buyers themselves. They just really want the house. But this roof could be a killer.

A full day goes by and you've haven't heard anything. The buyers are texting you. They're worried. They're young. They didn't expect homebuying to be this difficult and stressful. Well, it can be. Have patience.

You try the agent again. No answer.

You start to get mad. You leave both a voicemail and a text, politely enquiring about that buyer credit you discussed. You consider an email too but dismiss it as overkill, at least at this point. You wait some more.

Finally she calls you back. The seller is offering a credit for half the price of a new roof.

Huh, maybe you can work with this.

You get with the buyers and explain that the seller is meeting them halfway.

Can they handle the other half?

It turns out they can. One of their dads can lend them some cash. The work can be done after closing.

A few roofers come out for estimates, a price is decided, and all parties agree.

You saved the deal and ensured happy clients by doing the right thing. It took extra work. It caused you some stress. Yet you acted professionally. Your conscience is clear. Did you fend off the karma monster?

That's for you to decide. I like to believe you did.

DON'T BE A DICK

Some people are agents who really shouldn't be.

Simply put, if you can't get along well with other people, this isn't the lifestyle for you.

Agent/client relationships, that's one thing. But what about agent to agent? Peer to peer?

In any given region, at any given time, there are only so many properties available for the local agent population to work on. I'm talking about properties already listed in the MLS or for auction or FSBO, wherever. That's the inventory. Usually there are a lot more licensed agents in town than available homes. So there's a scramble, a fight, like kids when someone breaks the piñata at a party. It would be good to be a kid and know the guy who runs the piñata factory. Maybe you'd get some extra stuff the other kids wouldn't. It works like this in real estate too.

Say you have a buyer looking for a specific, hard-to-find kind of property. Then one appears on the market, listed with an agent you've never met or heard of. There's a good chance they've already marketed it amongst their inner circle even before it became public.

These are known as pocket listings.

As in, "Hey, I've got this house I'm gonna list next week. Got anyone for it?"

Over time you'll get some yourself and tell your friends about them. You'll feel so powerful, like you've got a secret from the world. It's all yours.

Unfortunately this one that just hit the market isn't yours, and you don't even know the agent. Your buyer is going crazy over it. You show it, they love it, it's offer time.

You call the agent to try and get some info on the place. Any offers? Anything you need to know that's not in the listing? They don't answer, so you leave a message. Later you try again. Still no answer. You leave another message, then try a text or email. All you're asking for is some simple information.

When three days go by with no reply, you figure, screw it, let's send in an offer anyway.

You squeeze the best offer you can out of your client and submit it with a 48-hour response deadline.

Then you wait some more.

(You could always try contacting the listing agent's broker and complain about his charge's poor communication skills, but you may just get silence there as well, since technically the agent hasn't done anything wrong.)

You wrote a good respectful offer. Just below list price, solid financing, no weird requests. You should be at least countered....

The deadline elapses. No counter, no rejection, no nothing. Your buyer is flabbergasted. This looks bad on you. Why don't you have any news?

You explain to him for the fourth time what's happening here. The listing agent is a jerk. He's trying to double-end it, which is agent-talk for scoring both buyer- and seller-side commission. This sour grape-flavored speculation doesn't comfort your client, who just wants a chance at the darn house. You almost want to go down to the office where that agent works and ring his neck. You swear that if you ever get a listing and that guy comes calling, you'll be a jerk right back to him, even though that's not how you operate. You'll make a special case for him.

When at last you notice the property has gone into contract, you check the details on it and see that the buyer's agent was someone in that guy's office, probably just down the hall from him. You don't know her either, but it doesn't matter. In-house deals happen all the time. Nothing illegal about them. But couldn't he just at least have had the human decency to send you a rejection? Anything? Jeez!

This really happens. So don't feel shaken the first time it happens to you.

This is a people business. The more people you know, the better. You more liked you are, the better.

I enjoy meeting other agents and getting deals done with them in a professional manner. Most of them are good honest people just trying to do their job and satisfy their clients. When you finish a deal with someone who knows their job and is an all-round pro, you want to do every deal with them. You hope to see their name on one of your contracts again soon. You ask yourself why every other agent can't be like that one, why some people have to be so impatient and rude and combative and noncommunicative. Escrows can be stressful enough with all the things that could go wrong. Why compound that stress by acting like a jackass?

It's hard to work toward a common goal with someone you can't stand.

Last year I had two back-to-back. The first kept sending me angry, screaming emails for no reason. The second phoned me every single day, multiple times per day, and seemed to be suffering from multiple personalities and memory lapses. It turned out they both had ownership interest in the properties they were selling and couldn't separate their emotions from the business side of things. Both gave me hell. My wonderful girlfriend put up with my daily reports of adventures with these imbeciles.

When my deal with the angry email guy finally closed, he actually sent me one more message saying it was a pleasure to have worked with me and that he hoped to do it again soon! I don't think he even realized the irony in this and how his behavior had affected our working relationship. I guess that's just the way he runs his life.

The second one, the phone call guy, met me at the property to hand me keys, shake my hand, and thank me for helping with the transaction. Again, just another day for him.

This must say something about me and my patience as an agent, or as a person in general. I know agents who would've never gotten those houses closed working with those guys. Both escrows would've blown up. Maybe it means I'm too patient. I do know I ended up with a happy seller on one property and a happy buyer on the other. And two nice commission checks.

Tolerance. That's the word.

As agents we have to be able to work together. But no one will want to work with you if you're impossible. As in any industry, reputations grow and spread. We all know who the good ones are -- and the bad ones. At least the ones who've been around for a while. You stay away from them if you can.

The new ones, you really have to watch out for.

Remember that everyone is your competition. This isn't like working in an office where each employee has his or her own job, a piece of the greater puzzle. In a real estate office, everyone is working toward the same goal, yes, but it's an individual goal.

Closing a property and getting paid.

Unless you're on some kind of hierarchical team, that new lady in the cubicle or desk next to yours isn't going to help you get that done.

Who knows, she may even try to sabotage you. Seriously.

She's new here, in from a big brokerage in Wisconsin. She's chatty and seems to know her stuff. She's looking for a buddy in the office, just as we all do in a strange place. You feel she's friendly enough so you chat back, laugh a bit, compare client pet-peeves. Eighties pop plays overhead. It's cool, the office is laid-back. Your work is going well.

The morning coffee starts to press on your bladder walls and you get up to go to the bathroom.

Unthinkingly you leave your laptop open or computer screen on. You could have sensitive information on display there. Client names, phone numbers, emails, property lists, whatever, it's there, and *she's* there.

You barely know her name, let alone her ethics. It's Thursday morning and the office is practically empty. She may be dry and need some leads or a quick check; the bills are coming. She could easily peek over at what you're working on and with whom. And the next thing you know, that buyer you've been struggling with for two months isn't returning your calls or texts anymore. What you don't know is he's working with her.

This is an extreme example, I know, but don't think it's never happened. Or couldn't happen. We're all kids fighting for that piñata candy, remember?

Because of this, many seasoned agents work alone in individual, personalized offices, or even from their homes. As long as you have a phone, a computer, and printer, you can get most things done. Your broker's office could just be where you hang, or maintain, your license.

Brand new agents who join large brokerages for training are usually grouped into cubicles or tiny desks, and they stay there until one day they realize they really don't have to be there. They can do their work anywhere they choose.

Good agent friendships are built over time through trust and respect, over deals made and results produced. A few days of cubicle talk won't cut it.

We all compete, yes, because we're competitors, whether we like it or not. Real estate is competition. Your days of having co-workers are over. Now you just have peers. Hundreds, maybe thousands, locally. Millions nationally.

Thankfully much more good than bad.

YOU CAN'T ALWAYS GET WHAT YOU WANT

Everybody wants a deal.

Whether you're shopping for groceries or clothes, appliances or electronics, holiday decorations or medical insurance, it's always the same: what's the best price?

The prices on those things are non-negotiable. They're set, take-it-or-leave-it. Of course there are a few exceptions. In my eighteen total years of retail, I actually did have a handful customers ask if we could give them a lower price on certain items due to damage or shelf wear. Sometimes it worked, sometimes it didn't, yet those folks were smart enough to know that if you don't ask for it, you won't get it.

In real estate the prices are indeed negotiable. You can ask for anything. Just remember, it's up to the market whether you get it or not.

I was taught that a house is worth what a buyer is willing to pay for it and what a seller is willing to take for it.

This is the essence of cash transactions, where no appraisal is required. Throw an appraiser in the mix and things may change a bit, but still the seller may decide to sell at the appraised value even if it's less than the agreed-upon purchase price. Buyers so love when this happens!

To get to that point, though, they still have to work to reach a purchase price acceptable to both parties.

This process can be very straightforward and easy:

"We love it! We'll offer full price!"

Or it can be difficult:

"Yeah, we like it, but we wanna start low and see what they say."

It's up to the two agents to craft the deal, based on what the local market's doing. If it's hot with low inventory, sellers have the advantage. If it's slow with a lot of houses sitting around, buyers have the edge. And despite what their agent tells them, clients don't always listen.

They're looking for a deal and they will get it!

A "deal" means different things to different people. The full-price offer lady – call her Betty – has a young family, is moving from Florida, and needs to find a home, like, yesterday.

Real estate is crazy in her new city. Her price range is tight with very few properties for sale. Buyers are bidding them up. Her agent shows Betty and her hubby a dozen homes and they fall for a heavily-dated dollhouse with a large lot. It just hit the market but needs lots of work. I mean, lots. The price reflects that. The lot is superb, with extra parking and room for their kids and dogs to play. There's even space for a pool if they wanted that down the line.

They're up for the work inside. The husband has done some contracting and plumbing during the past few years, so he's ready. They've found their place.

They don't blink at the price. They don't even try to knock it down because they know that wasting time could cost them the house. They understand. They go in full price on the first day and get the property. They're thrilled. Then their agent so keenly reminds them that once the house is fixed up and remodeled, it could be the jewel of the block.

"What a deal you guys got!"

On the other hand, you've got a buyer, Zach. He will only buy at his price. Warnings of a sellers' market don't faze him. In his mind, the buyer's always in control.

He locates a home he likes and checks it out with his agent. Again, the property is fresh, just listed. The yard features a spectacular pebble-tech waterfall pool –– he loves those –– plus an additional garage out back for extra cars and toys. Loves that too. He's just divorced and needs an awesome bachelor pad of his own. Inside there's a full bar and a theater room, plus a game room upstairs with a pool table that's included in the sale. The balcony off the master overlooks that awesome backyard and the northern mountains in the distance. Downstairs there's a chef's kitchen with top-of-the-line appliances and a flashy backsplash.

This place would work just fine.

"Overpriced," he mutters.

Prepared for this very moment, you whip out a list of sold comps. "Actually, for what you get here, it's right in line."

Zach studies the data a minute. He knows they're just numbers. He can beat them. Surely the seller must be desperate to sell.

He spits out an offer.

"That's pretty low," you reply.

He knows the house will most likely sell for list price or very close to it. "Well, let's give it a try."

He's got nothing to lose.

Later in the day you get the offer signed and submitted to the listing agent.

Two days later: rejected.

Zach is astounded. "They didn't even counter?"

"Wanna try higher?"

"Nah, never mind. Too much."

So goes buyer Zach.

Eventually he'll get a house. He'll get his price. That's what getting a deal means to him. His price, his terms. The only thing is, how many agents will he burn through to get there? And how much will prices rise in the meantime?

Sellers want deals too. They want the most money for their homes. "My house sold for above appraisal! What a deal!"

If pricing a home is left up to me, I like to list it just a hair above the latest comps. That way there's room for negotiation and ideally the seller won't feel undersold and the buyer won't feel oversold.

Negotiations can be difficult. They teach whole classes on the subject. Books have been written on it. There's nothing like the psychological heat of a fiery negotiation. Two sides, buyer and seller, pulling in opposite directions, both looking to one-up the other, with their two agents as mediators.

As an agent, you have to be careful not to get emotionally involved. You have to stay coolly detached. Easy to say, hard to do.

You want to get that offer accepted for your buyer. He'll be happy and if all goes well, you'll get paid. And you want to get paid for all the trouble and hard work you've been putting in with him. The other agent probably feels the same way. Maybe she wants to get that house sold so she can help her seller buy another -- and get paid twice.

What's the motivation?

Your buyer could be a cold cash investor. They only look at numbers. They don't get caught up in sentimental things such as having enough room to grow with their family. They're going to rent the place out for income. One deal doesn't work, they go on to the next one, because there's always another house or building. They have a max they can spend on a given property and that's it. They're emotionally detached, so why shouldn't you be?

Investors don't fall prey to the pleasure and pain method, which every good agent should use. Take Zach from above. Sooner or later he's going to find a place he just can't pass up and he'll actually make an offer high enough to be entertained and countered.

The negotiation begins. He doesn't like the counter. Still too high. He's in control. That seller needs to see things from his (Zach's) view.

You're his agent. You resist getting heated over this.

"Do you really like the house?" you ask. "Do you really want it? I mean, we can go look at these others."

You're sort of taking it away from him. It's like the house is on a boat drifting away from the shore, leaving Zach to watch helplessly. Unless, that is, he's willing to raise his offer and go try to catch it.

His love of the property is the pleasure; his risk of losing it is the pain.

It's his decision. What's more important? Paying a bit more to secure the home of his dreams? Or standing firm and letting it go because he didn't think it was a good enough deal?

It's maddening to see what people put themselves through over money.

Some sellers feel their homes are made of gold. These gilded palaces can't be compared to anything else, especially to the comp down the street, that exact model-match that sold three weeks ago. No way. Roger the seller doesn't want to hear that. His is special. And he'll list it alright, he'll put it out there.

"But I'm not taking any less than...."

Okay, step back.

You're the agent. Do you want this listing?

How bad does Roger really want to sell his house? What are his motivations and goals?

A lot of agents will take a listing they know won't sell as long as they can place a For Sale sign out front.

At any given time the MLS is crowded with overpriced listings 100, 200 days old. Or more.

The agents would like to sell them, for sure, but since folks like Roger won't budge on their unrealistic prices, they'll be content with letting their signs do some self-marketing for them. They get calls and collect new buyers and sellers that way.

I've had clients ask me about certain properties they see while driving around.

"That one's under contract," I report.

"Then how come they still have the sign out there?"

"They keep it up till the house closes. In case it comes back on the market."

"Well, that's deceiving!"

Or this:

"That house has had a sign on it for over a year."

I reply, "Looks like it's priced too high for the area."

"If they can't sell it, why do they keep the sign up?"

Again, it's just marketing. If you have a stubborn seller and you can't sell the house, you may as well sell yourself.

Ask a hundred agents and see who'd rather have five $200K listings than one $1M listing. The commission to sell either would be the same. More would go with the five. Cheaper homes sell faster. There are more buyers for them. Plus often the more expensive homes are in exclusive neighborhoods that place limitations on sale signs or even open houses, eliminating some of your marketing power.

The big fancy listing is nice to have. It may give your brand an air of elegance. But it's not worth anything to you until you close it.

Big or small, a house is a house, and a paycheck is a paycheck.

In the end, stubborn Roger may not really want to sell. He's reaching for something that's not there. Buyers aren't suckers. Usually.

As his agent, at least you won't have to parade him around to a stream of houses he has no intention of buying. You can carry on with your other work while he sits in his family room with no offers to entertain. If the sign is working and you're getting calls, you're doing OK. If, however, he won't allow the sign and wants way too much price-wise, maybe a different seller, with a different property, will be more worth your time.

Another example would be seller Seth, who's facing more pressure but can't see beyond dollar signs.

Seth's got a place he's remodeled in a popular area of the city. He'd intended to stay there, but something life-changing has occurred. His girlfriend Heather, who's in the military, has been transferred out of state.

He feared this would happen. He obviously wants to stay with her. She's quickly lined up an agent in the new city and is checking out homes there, sending him photos and videos. He's even visited once to look too. He's not crazy about the architecture there or even the city itself, and if not for Heather – maybe someday his wife – he'd never move there. But this is his situation.

The couple's agent has informed them that no serious seller will entertain an offer from them if Seth hasn't already accepted an offer on his property back home.

A few weeks go by. He gets lots of showings, even a few offers, which he rejects as too low. He's put too much cash into the house to let it go like that, he says. Plus he and Heather don't have anywhere to go yet after selling, so there's no real pressure yet.

Yet.

You want Seth to get the most for his house. You see him sweating over it. You know the house is priced a little high. You hear it from buyers and other agents. The sold comps can barely reach it. It's a very popular area, though. Given time, this place will sell.

Then Seth gets the call from Heather. She's found the ultimate home for them. She has to have this house. It's got everything she's always wanted. Etc, etc, etc.

On the same day, an offer on Seth's house comes rolling in. The best one yet. Cash too.

Now, you wanna talk about pressure?

You'd think that Seth would be ready to work a deal at this point.

"Still too low," he complains.

"Let's counter it."

He agrees, reluctantly.

As you send it over to the buyer's agent, you don't feel good about it. Still too high.

You get a call from the agent. She explains that the buyer feels his original offer is more than generous and won't be budging.

You think to yourself, does Heather know any of this is going on?

You get back to Seth and give him the news.

It's doesn't go well.

"Screw 'em then!" he reacts.

You try to talk reason. The offer is cash and can close quickly. A similar financed offer probably wouldn't appraise. A new house, a new life, is waiting. Heather is waiting.

And there's Seth, torn between reuniting with his girlfriend and getting the maximum dollar for his old house.

He won't give in, so the offer expires.

Two days later you get a call. It's Seth. He sounds a bit more reasonable. He gives you a lowered figure and asks if you think the buyer will go for it. You turn around and run it by the buyer's agent.

Nope. He's already out looking at other homes. The opportunity is slipping away. You knew it would.

Pleasure and pain for Seth.

Another two days pass. Seth again:

"Ok, I'll take the offer. I'll take it. Let them know."

You do your thing and talk to the agent. Uh oh -- her buyer's moved on to another house. They don't want Seth's anymore.

Got a better deal elsewhere.

You know what's coming next.

Heather's dream house? Gone in a week.

Who knows if the buyer got a deal, but it doesn't matter. Seth and Heather are back where they were a week before. No offer, nowhere to go.

Which leaves you stranded too.

No deal.

Somehow you knew it was going to end up this way with Seth. Same with Zach.

Roger too. No sale.

It seems that the same people who practically wretch at the idea of paying full price when they're buying something are the same ones who insist on full price when selling something!

And they're so driven by the idea of the deal, they quite often miss out on it.

Back when the housing market crashed, fantastic properties could be had for fantastic prices, especially in Las Vegas. Certain buyers I met back then hesitated to make a move. They expected prices to keep dropping further.

Eventually a slow recovery began. Values started to increase.

They hesitated still.

Every month, the health of real estate improved just a little more.

They ignored it. Wouldn't believe it.

Today, with the market on fire both locally and nationally, some of those individuals remain on the sidelines.

Prices are too high for them now!

You, the agent, can only shake your head and laugh.

The deal of a lifetime was right in front of them.

BE SAFE

While working with the public you'll encounter all kinds of personalities and temperaments. You've seen some of the "friends" I've met along the way. Truth is, you never know what could be coming at you at any particular time.

A few years ago I worked in an office of about nine agents. At least two of them carried.

Guns.

On their hips, concealed under long buttoned-up shirts.

Perfectly legal in Nevada. Two of the best guys in the world too. Always laughing, great attitudes, real pros at their work. And big guys. Kick your butt by just overpowering you with their size. You wouldn't want to challenge them anyway.

One day one of them was attacked going into a vacant house.

It was a normal day. He was out with a buyer. They went to an empty bank-owned property. He got the key out of the box and opened the door.

Bam! Someone whacked him in the head with a baseball bat. He went down. People in the house ran out the back. The buyer had to call for help.

The poor guy recovered but never forgot. What a frightening thing to go through! Now he's cautious when he opens doors, and he's ready.

His office mate hasn't suffered the same experience, but he's prepared for it. As we all should be.

I'm not saying all agents should carry firearms for protection. It's just that safety is something to always keep in mind.

Just imagine you're alone in an empty house with someone and something doesn't feel right. I've been there. I had those experiences with Mr. 5000 and Curt the angry homeowner. You get the feeling fast. You just want to get out of there.

Agent safety is a legitimate concern. Every year, dozens of agents are hurt or even murdered by people posing as buyers or sellers. Think about it: you may have made an appointment to meet someone for the first time in a vacant house in a strange neighborhood. Criminals look for these kinds of opportunities.

You're there waiting and your new client shows up. He's very tall and bald and seems kind of dodgy. He doesn't say much. He glances around the front of the property first, then comes inside and not only closes but locks the door behind him. Weird. Now you're alone with him.

You realize maybe you should've met him at a coffee shop first and checked his ID or something like that.

You stay cool and show him around like you would any other client. He darts from room to room as though looking for someone or something. You're a bit hesitant to head upstairs, but you do.

He acts the same way up there. Minimal comments, rapid movements, crazy eyes. You start to realize he's just a quiet intense guy. An investor apparently. He's not interested in you. He only cares about making money on the house.

You finish the tour and he heads out as quickly as he came in. Says he'll be in touch.

"Be in touch?" you almost say aloud.

Later that afternoon he calls you and says he wants to offer on the house. You follow through and his offer gets accepted. Now you get to go through an escrow with him!

Clearly this is something good that could've gone the other way and been really bad.

Open houses can be risky.

Anyone can come in. Anyone.

Unless there's lots of activity from neighbors or interested parties, agents are often alone inside the house, and yes, vulnerable. Anything can happen.

Someone like the tall dodgy investor could wander in. Only this guy's not an investor. He's a killer. Or a rapist. And since you're such a good advertiser, putting yourself out there just like you should to build your business, you found his radar and he's been following you secretly for months. He noticed you'll be at this house today from 12 to 4.

You're alone when he shows up and shuts the door behind him. He heads toward you. You immediately sense there's a problem.

What would you do?

A good way to avoid situations like this is to do open houses with team or lending partners. Lenders are always happy and willing to participate because they're looking for new clients too. People aiming to cause harm are likely to stay away if they know the agent isn't alone on the property.

Doorknocking can be done in pairs as well. Religious and charitable groups do this. Why? For safety. Mischievous homeowners and tenants are less apt to harass a group than a single individual (of course, there's a greater chance they won't open the door!).

Initial meetings with new buyers or even sellers can take place in neutral places such as an office or coffee shop. There you can make contact with a person or persons and make sure they are who they said they were over the phone or in an email. If they refuse to show, then maybe they aren't as serious about doing business with you as they seemed.

Or maybe they weren't interested in business at all.

In the case of my friend who was attacked at the vacant property, that was an unfortunate incident that could've happened to any of us. You've heard it said that bad things happen to good people all the time. Good people just trying to be successful by helping others. These days it seems someone is always out there looking to take advantage of someone else.

When you were a child, your parents, just like mine, taught you not to speak to strangers. Now you do it for a living!

4. HOW DOES IT WORK?

LISA'S ESCROW

They say that no two snowflakes are the same.

The same can be said for these things called escrows.

Escrow is the process through which property is conveyed from seller to buyer. To outsiders it's a mysterious time full of unknowns.

First-time homebuyers are downright frightened by it. Brand new agents both pine for it and fear it at the same time. To experienced real estate agents it's a mere series of steps to getting their latest deals closed.

But they can't do it alone. They'll have lots of help along the way.

This is what the new agent has to realize.

During my early years in retail management, I always wanted to do everything myself. That way I knew it would get done right. My store manager wanted certain tasks completed on a given day and he'd leave me a list. Sometimes a long list. And the day is only so long.

The store would get busy. I'd run into other responsibilities with employees and customers and vendors. Time would zip by. Meanwhile the list would sit, unfinished, maybe even un-started.

This couldn't continue. I would have to learn to delegate.

At first it was hard splitting up the list, deciding which employee would get which task.

Ask any control freak to split up his daily duties and spread them out amongst other workers he doesn't fully trust and you'll see what I mean.

Yet I had to do it. It was the only way to manage successfully. Once I began to do things this way, I became free to manage the store and make sure others were doing the work correctly.

Now as an agent, I'm the manager of my deals. I have partners who aid me in different aspects of the escrow process. I check in with them periodically to see how things are going on their end; meanwhile I'm able to keep up with my own duties. I don't need to feel overwhelmed because I have a good professional team I can trust, who knows what they're doing. Even when a deal goes haywire!

Let's look at Lisa, a new agent with one of those high-powered lunch-money firms in Las Vegas. She's been licensed for three months and hasn't done any deals yet. Until now. She just got her buyer Max's offer accepted.

Over the next thirty or so days – her buyer's contract will specify an estimated closing date – she'll be in varying degrees of contact with several people:

1. Max, her buyer
2. Olivia, Max's lender (loan officer) and her team
3. Kendra, the title officer at the title company handling the escrow, and Kendra's team
4. Jose, the listing agent for the home Max is purchasing
5. Aaron, a home inspector
6. Damian, an appraiser
7. Beth, a transaction coordinator
8. Kim, Lisa's team leader

There could be others if needed, such as an attorney or even the brokers of the companies where Lisa and Jose work. Outside handymen or specialists like roofers or pool guys may be called upon. Or maybe the county assessor. Perhaps a therapist for Lisa.

Just kidding. Lisa will be fine as long as she follows up with everyone and makes sure they're all doing their part. She knows that Max will come to her with any issues and that she'll need to find ways to smooth them out.

She knows this because she's been told so by her team leader Kim. Kim will be her safety net in case a disaster should come along. Otherwise she'll let Lisa attempt to handle things on her own, like watching as a child crosses the street alone for the first time.

Or as an amateur trapeze artist braves a tightrope.

Yeah, more like that.

If only Max knew the truth. He doesn't know this is Lisa's very first escrow and that she's scared out of her gourd. Sure, he knows she's a newer agent, but not *that* new. Lisa would never tell him that, at least not voluntarily. She wants him to feel confident in her. She needs him to feel assured that she can handle all aspects of his purchase from beginning to end.

Look, everybody has to start somewhere, right? Everybody has to be someone's first whatever at some point. What about a lawyer and his first case? People usually look for experienced attorneys. They fear a new one might make mistakes and cause them to lose a trial. People look for experienced real estate agents too for the same reason. Errors and oversights can wreck deals. No one wants to give the rookie a chance.

But Max likes Lisa, and she likes him. He's an older gentleman in his mid-sixties with a bald crown and a high waistline buying a cheap townhouse after a few years of renting. Lisa's a young woman in her mid-twenties with a chestnut bob and a pencil skirt trying to make sure her client's townhouse dream becomes a reality. They became entwined through Kim's lead-generating system and have a good working relationship. He's very satisfied with her performance so far. Heck, she just got his full-price offer accepted on that dump downtown. Her lack of experience hasn't resulted in any problems yet. And she wants to keep it that way.

So she turns to Kim. "What do I do now?!"

Busy Kim smiles and asks her if she's looked back at her notes from training – specifically the lesson entitled, "Escrow".

Lisa turns red and says no.

"It's all there. Check it out."

Lisa goes to her car and retrieves the thick binder of papers she amassed during her training classes. Back in the office she finds an empty desk and sits down to review.

She has several things to do.

The key here is Max's accepted purchase agreement, the document, or "contract", everyone involved in the transaction will be working from.

Lisa's notes tell her she needs to get that vital paperwork into the hands of Max's lender Olivia so she and her assistants can start working on Max's loan. Olivia will in turn contact an appraisal company to send an appraiser out to the house to perform an appraisal.

Lisa reads further. Next in line, it seems, is Kendra, the title officer. She'll need a copy of Max's contract too. Kendra will "open escrow", which means she'll start a file for this transaction. Everything relating to the transfer of property between the seller and Max will take place here.

If the escrow itself were a person, it would live at Title, probably sleeping under a desk somewhere.

Lisa hasn't met Olivia or Kendra yet, but she'll get to know them well, if only through phone calls and email, over the next month. They've already worked with Kim several times and will be more than happy to help Lisa succeed with her first sale. They want her repeat business, and Kim's as well.

Lisa already knows Beth, an hourly employee who sits in a corner of Kim's office. She's their transaction coordinator. She will make sure Max's file of all necessary paperwork is complete by closing so that Lisa and Kim can get paid.

She's their right-hand woman.

A copy of Max's contract will go to her too.

Lisa looks for Kim, finds her in the lunchroom, and double checks with her to make sure her notes are correct and that she's understanding the process so far.

With a mouthful of bagel and cream cheese, Kim gives her a thumbs-up.

Lisa heads back to her computer and sends out the paperwork in three separate emails to Olivia, Kendra, and Beth.

Eventually she'll streamline this and shoot her contracts to all three in the same email.

Baby steps.

Before she forgets, she writes to Jose, the listing agent, and gives him the contact info for Olivia, Kendra, and Beth.

What else?

Oh yeah, Max.

She scans her notes again and gives him a call. He answers, as always. He's thrilled to hear from her.

"We opened escrow today," she happily reports.

"Great! What's next?"

She stumbles a moment, not expecting that question, but recovers.

"We'll need to do an inspection on the house."

"When's that?"

"Um...my transaction coordinator is setting it up. I'll be letting you know."

They chat for a few minutes. He informs her he has a doctor's appointment on Wednesday at 10, so he won't be available then. She lets him know he'll be hearing from Olivia regarding any paperwork she'll need him to sign. When the conversation is over, she falls back in her chair and lets out a big breath. She made it through.

She led him to believe she knows exactly what she's doing.

She gazes at the ceiling, then remembers something. She forgot to mention Max's deposit on the house. The earnest money deposit. The EMD. $1500. It has to be at title within two business days, per the contract.

She calls him back. She explains that Kendra will be sending him wiring instructions and that he can take them to his bank and—

"I'll write 'em a check," he proclaims. "What's the address? I'll drop it off."

Being new, Lisa isn't sure if title will accept a personal check for the EMD. She only hears talk of electronic wires.

She hesitantly agrees, gets off the phone, and rushes to consult with Kim.

Yes, they take checks.

Another deep breath for Lisa.

It won't be the last.

Max takes not two but three business days to run his check over to Kendra's office – just long enough for Kendra and Jose to start asking Lisa where the EMD is. She contacts Max and he apologizes for the delay: he's been "busy".

On the fifth day after the acceptance of the offer, Max and Lisa meet Aaron, the home inspector, at the property for an inspection. Lisa and Aaaon are on time; Max is late.

The property, a single-story townhouse, is a relic of the mid-1970s and looks it. The $90,000 price tag reflects the shabby condition and downtown area. As does the SOLD AS-IS disclaimer in the listing. But Max is okay with it. He's been living in the heart of the city for several years and feels comfortable there. As for the retro wallpaper, popcorned ceilings, and spicy-mustard-yellow appliances, all will be phased out over time. For the time being, they're livable. Max just wants to get in. He's already given notice at his apartment.

While Aaron is doing his thing, Lisa asks Max about the paperwork Beth sent him in his email.

"I didn't get nothing," he says.

"Did you check your spam?"

"Nah, that's all junk."

"Take a look, it could be there."

"What is it anyway?"

She's not quite sure, she can't remember. (She makes a mental note to acquaint herself better with this paperwork.) She knows it's stuff from the seller as well as forms from her office. All mandatory items. He needs to sign them for Beth's file. And signing electronically is easy, she tells him. You just follow the prompts on the screen.

"Eh, computers and me, we don't always see eye to eye," he chuckles. She reassures him it won't be difficult. She's done it herself and it's easy. She reminds him to check his spam.

Aaron finishes up and they go over the findings of the inspection.

Lotta little things, three big things.

The roof has a leak. The air conditioner isn't blowing cold enough. And the water heater is old and showing signs of leakage and corrosion.

Max is alarmed. "Seller's gonna fix that shit, right?"

Lisa freezes. She's never seen Max get upset like this. He's forgetting about the as-is part of the deal. She needs to chill him out. "We can ask, let me speak with the listing agent."

"The hell with asking, demand it!"

Lisa and Aaron lock eyes. This is going badly with Max.

"I imagine something can be worked out," Aaron chimes in calmly.

"Hope so!" Max blurts out.

The mood is ruined. Aaron completes his presentation and says he'll have the full report over to them within 24 hours. He grabs his laptop and clipboard and slips out the door, leaving Max and Lisa alone.

They scatter quickly, coldly, with few words, an upset client and an inexperienced agent. Lisa gets in her car with a lump in her throat. She's worried. This inspection could threaten her first deal. Max might be angry with her, even though it isn't her fault.

She goes back to the office and limps in to see Kim. She tells her all about it. Her eyes even tear up a bit.

Turns out, she has options. Maybe the seller will agree to give Max a repair credit. Perhaps the seller has a home warranty on the property. If Max buys a home warranty through escrow, as many buyers do, it'll be there for him to use for these repairs after closing. And maybe the seller will even pay for it.

Or perhaps the appraisal will require the seller to make the repairs in order to close the property.

Kim turns to Beth. "Has the appraisal been ordered yet?"

"Haven't heard. I'll email Olivia."

Kim instructs Lisa to check with Olivia too. It's been five days. Follow up, follow up.

She calls. Appraisal not ordered yet. Max hasn't signed the required paperwork. He'd made an appointment a few days back to visit Olivia's office but then canceled and said he'd need to reschedule. She hasn't heard from him.

Lisa can't handle talking to him right now, even though she needs to. The wounds of the day are still fresh. She starts to feel angry that he's acting this way.

Didn't he want to a buy a house? Why is he ignoring his lender? Why did he get upset at the inspection when he knew the house was being sold as-is? Is he going to cancel the deal and waste her time?

To cool off she goes to the Starbucks around the corner from the office and gets a Frappuccino©. She holes up in a corner with her laptop and wades through other leads. Motivated buyers. Motivated sellers. None of this wishy-washy crap.

Her phone rings. It's Max.

She's afraid to answer it. Could be bad news. He could be mad still.

It goes to voicemail.

She takes a drag on her drink and listens to the message with the sound turned low, so no one else around can hear it.

"Hey Lisa, it's uh, it's Max. I uh, [loud cough] y'know uh, I'm really sorry...."

He feels bad about losing his temper earlier. Says his hip's been bothering him and he forgot to take a pain med. He wants to meet with her to get everything signed and move ahead with the property. Does she know anyone who can perform the repairs?

Wow. Suddenly she feels so much better. Poor Max and his sore hip, he was having a bad day. She needs to respond so he knows she's okay.

She waits a few minutes, then gives him a call. He's ecstatic to hear from her and super apologetic. She tells him it's alright, she understands, she didn't know about his hip. She'll look into options regarding the repairs and let him know what can be done. He thanks her profusely. The conversation is like a giant verbal hug. The tension, the gnawing discomfort, is gone.

Later that afternoon she stops by his apartment with Beth's paperwork and he signs all of it. It's hot, so he offers her a popsicle, which she accepts. She slips in a friendly reminder for him to get back in touch with Olivia. He declares he'll do that first thing in the morning.

All is well.

Just before dusk she departs with a smile and a wave and heads home for a relaxed happy dinner with her boyfriend Ben, who gets to hear all about her escapades with Max.

In the morning she's charged up. Kim has some new buyers for her to meet. They're preapproved and ready to look at homes after work. But first things first.

She checks in with Jose about the possibility of a home warranty or a repair credit, and he says he'll look into it.

Olivia emails her and reports that she's met with Max and can push ahead with ordering the appraisal.

Kendra at title notifies her that she's working on clearing a judgment against the seller of Max's place for some unpaid HOA dues. Lisa looks concerned, but Beth says it's common and nothing to be alarmed about. Kendra will handle it.

With Max's situation under control for now, Lisa takes the rest of the morning off from it to concentrate on looking up listings and setting up showing appointments for her new clients. Her confidence is growing. She's learning. She'll actually know what to do now if – no, when – she gets these latest buyers into contract.

When Aaron's inspection report hits Lisa's inbox, Kim loosely instructs her on how to write up a request for repairs and/or a repair credit. Unsure of herself she creeps away to attempt it, then comes back to show Kim and Beth her work. They all have a good, stress-relieving laugh.

Her verbiage is pretty crude, she admits.

If only Max knew how green she was!

Beth types it up properly on the correct form and emails it to Jose. Lisa, ever the note taker, will use it as a template for future requests.

Max calls and complains to her about his drive to Olivia's office and how someone almost hit him in an intersection. Why can't her office be closer to his apartment? It can't and it just isn't, but oh well, what're you gonna do? Oh, and his hip feels a lot better today, by the way. He thanks her again for coming by with the papers and asks if she has any updates. Not yet, but he'll be the first to know, she assures him. He keeps her on the phone for twenty minutes. Finally she tells him she's got a training meeting to attend and he happily relents. Set free, she shakes her head and gets up to walk around the office a bit. Max is quite a case!

She spends the next two days, through the weekend, working with the new buyers. They like some of what they're seeing but aren't quite ready yet to make offers. They haven't seen the right place for them. No sweat. Lisa knows how it goes. She'll keep working at it.

Jose finally responds.

The seller has no home warranty and won't make repairs, but he'll give a repair credit at closing. $1000. This is good. Max will like it.

She and Beth announce this credit in a small addendum to the contract and send it to both buyer and seller to sign. With Lisa's help over the phone, Max figures out how to sign and resend an e-document. He's happy. She emails the completed addendum to Olivia and Kendra to add to her files.

Success. They got past the inspection issue.

Later Max calls again. Lisa is out with her clients but excuses herself and answers. He's really upset.

Olivia's asked him for additional paperwork relating to his divorce.

"That was three years ago!" he shouts. "What the hell's she want that for?"

How should Lisa know? She's not the lender.

She won't say that, of course.

"Did you ask why she needs it?" she enquires instead.

"No! It's not important. I ain't giving her that."

"Okay. Relax. I'll talk to her."

"There's no reason she needs that shit."

"Okay Max, I'll call her."

"You tell her I'll go somewhere else."

Lisa feels her head getting hot. "Max, breathe."

"Wh—I'm breathing fine! You tell her she can stuff it."

He hangs up.

She pulls her phone away from her ear and peers at it blankly, speechlessly, for a moment. She's shaking. This guy's gonna give her a mental breakdown.

Meanwhile she has clients waiting in the other room.

She might need another Frappuccino©.

On the way back to the office she gets a hold of Olivia. Apparently she'd requested -- for the third time -- Max's divorce decree and a record of his child support payments for his teenage son. That was all she needed. He'd gotten her everything else. All debt, or lack of debt, had to be reported. This was home lending, post-Recession, 2000-teens. Full disclosure, extra caution, nothing unusual. Just the rules, ma'am. Or sir.

Max's loan wouldn't be able to proceed without this information.

Lisa waits till later in the evening, around 8:30, to call Max. She's had dinner and changed into her pj's: a tanktop and a pair of Ben's boxers. She's relaxed on the couch. She's armed with information. She's readied herself for a fight but figures it'll be more like a therapy session.

And it is.

Max goes into the details about his divorce and his son, who's now seventeen. Lisa listens empathetically and lets him talk. It's an uncomfortable subject for him. That's why he got so mad at Olivia. Lisa speaks slowly and tells him she understands. She explains that Olivia isn't trying to pry into his private life just for kicks. He's trying to get a home loan. Sometimes the guidelines require sensitive information. Olivia's trying to do her job. She can't do it without his cooperation.

The descent of evening darkness, combined with Lisa's gentle voice and open ear, works to soothe him. He begins to understand. He apologizes yet again for overreacting.

When the conversation is over, Lisa slumps into the couch and exhales hard.

Ben has been lounging nearby the whole time. "Babe, that was masterful."

She stares at the ceiling fan spinning above. She's spent. She's taking tomorrow off, for sure. She needs it.

She uses the time to clean her apartment and do laundry, good busy activities that allow the mind to rest and recover. Kim sends her a new lead to work on, a couple coming in from California. Cash buyers. Woohoo!

Meanwhile Max gets quiet. Too quiet.

Three days go by and no calls. No complaints, no raging questions. Not even any hip news. Lisa is busy with her other clients, so it's actually a blessing. She meets with the Californians and even writes and submits an offer for the buyers she's been working with for the last week and a half. They've found what they think is the perfect place for them – an unexpected choice that both surprised and delighted Lisa. She'd thought they didn't like the place.

On the fourth day, while she waits to hear back on the offer, things slow down a bit. She starts to wonder about Max. Not that she wants to get into a random discussion with him about nothing in particular, but something tells her she should call.

No answer. She leaves a message, stating that everything's okay and that she just wanted to say hello.

Olivia hasn't heard from him either since he got her the divorce paperwork.

Weird. Maybe he left town for a few days. Maybe he's not feeling well. Maybe...maybe anything!

"Just let it ride," Kim advises. People disappear and come back all the time. No need to panic.

The office is submerged in a mid-afternoon lull when two troubling emails show up almost simultaneously.

The first, sad news that Lisa's buyers' offer has been rejected by the sellers.

Which means Lisa is tasked with telling her clients their perfect home has gone to someone else. That's always hard.

The second, from Olivia, word that the appraisal on Max's place came in $5000 lower than the contract price.

Which means they'll have to renegotiate on price if the seller won't come down to the appraisal value. This is scary because she hasn't been in this situation before.

Double whammy, right in the face.

But no sense in delaying things.

Lisa texts the appraisal info to Jose and calls her buyers, who don't answer.

You don't leave this kind of news in a voicemail. You say, "Call me." She learned that early in her training.

The Californians have picked some properties to see, so she puts aside the dramas of the day to go show half a dozen lovely mansions with healthy price tags in the popular southwest part of town.

That's therapy for agents: the promise of something big when everything else seems to be crumbling.

The southwest homes are spectacular, the kind that Lisa herself dreams of owning someday. While her doing her job, she feels like she's in one of those TV shows that spotlight luxury properties. The clients are entertaining and easy-going, clearly happy with each other and excited about the future. Being with them reminds Lisa why she got into real estate in the first place – to have this kind of experience and be able to profit from it.

After the tour, the buyers invite her to dinner and she accepts (notifying Ben with a text). They find a superb Italian restaurant with authentic ambiance and a singing waiter. Lisa has more wine than usual and has to eat a lot of pasta and bread to smother it.

Hours go by.

Lights take effect.

The cheesecake is otherworldly.

In the dark but well-illuminated parking lot they exchange hugs and thank-you's and the customary "We'll be in touch!" salutations as two of them prepare to head back to California in the morning and the other to her little apartment twenty minutes north.

There's a voicemail from Jose that came in during dinner. Lisa's ignored it until now. She's still sitting in her car in the parking lot. Within a minute, reality has come raging back into her life. She nervously presses play and listens.

Just what she feared. The seller won't drop the price to $85,000, the appraised value. Contract price is $90,000. They're $5000 apart. That's a lot of money on a small purchase. He'll do $88,000, says Jose.

If Max refuses to raise his offer above $85,000, it could kill the entire deal.

Lisa can't let this happen. She's put too much into it already. There's got to be a fix.

From the front seat of her car, in a strange parking lot at 9 PM, she reaches out to Jose and they discuss the matter.

The $1000 repair credit is still on the table, if Max will go up to $88,000. Otherwise it's gone. Jose insists the appraisal was bad anyway and is looking to challenge it. He's contacted Damian, the appraiser, and sent him sold comps he says support the $90,000 price. He invites Lisa to do the same. If they can get the numbers revised, they won't have to renegotiate. She's all for that.

She doesn't tell him she hasn't heard from her talkative buyer in four days. He doesn't need to know that. Instead she asks for Damian's number so they can work together on this appraisal problem because, yeah, she's done this a million times!

During their talk, a text has come in from her buyers regarding their offer and her "Call me" message.

She calls and gives them the news.

The wife cries. The husband protests. "But we put in full price! How much did they get?"

"That's not -- they won't tell us that."

"Call them, we'll beat it."

"You can't, they already accepted the offer."

"I can't believe this!"

"But they're holding yours as a backup. In case the other one falls out. It happens a lot."

"Well it wouldn't happen with ours! We're solid."

"I'm so sorry, it's just – it's up to the seller--"

"Yeah and that goddamn listing agent so she can get more commission. This is a joke!"

Yikes. Meet Lisa the punching bag. What a day.

By the time she's done consoling this guy and his wife, the parking lot is empty and the restaurant has closed. Ben is texting, wondering where she is. It's too late to call Damian. Too late to do anything but cruise home and wonder why the universe is playing these cruel games with her right now.

She's not prepared for Max's "return". Especially the way he carries it out.

It's late morning. Lisa, Kim, and Beth are in Kim's office discussing the bad appraisal and the anguished buyers' failed offer, as well as the merry dinner with the Californians.

A newly-hired front desk receptionist knocks on the open door holding a bouquet of yellow roses. They all stare at her, dumbfounded.

"Lisa?" she searches.

"That's me."

She hands her the flowers.

"There's a card," says Beth.

Lisa opens it and reads: "Dear Lisa, had a medical scare but recovering now. All's well. Talk in a few weeks. Max."

Beth gasps. "Dead deal."

Kim says nothing. For once she's speechless, without an answer. Lisa knows what she has to do.

It's a touchy situation. Sick clients require finesse. Luckily she has it.

She gets in the car and drives across town to Max's apartment.

He's at home. At first he doesn't want to let her in, then allows it. He's walking slowly and speaking more quietly than usual. She can tell he's been through something. He offers her some water but she says no, she's fine. She takes a seat on the couch as he eases himself into a recliner.

Then they talk. Agent to client, human to human. Even in his weakened state he dominates the exchange, and she lets him.

He explains how he was at a shoe store when he started feeling dizzy and numb on one side of his face. Things got worse, an ambulance came. Next thing he knew he was at the hospital. They ran tests and kept him there overnight. In the morning his doctor told him he'd had a minor stroke. They wanted to keep him for two more days to monitor his condition. He agreed and ended up sleeping a great amount of the time. They'd just released him yesterday. He has new prescriptions to take and a follow-up appointment with the doctor in two weeks. He feels embarrassed that it happened and that he left Lisa in the dark.

"Don't be ridiculous!" she replies. "You're okay, that's what's important."

"Aw, you're too nice."

They chat a bit more before reaching the subject of real estate. She smartly and patiently lets him bring it up.

He still wants to move ahead with the townhouse. In fact he has to, he's got nowhere else to go. She was hoping to hear that. So with tact and a quiet tone she fills him in about the appraisal.

"I thought we agreed on ninety grand," he says.

"You did. But it appraised at eighty-five."

"That's good for me then."

"Well, yes. But no."

"Huh?"

She's trying not to get him worked up. He always seems to lose it when he disagrees with something. She even takes the opportunity to tell him so. This sudden gentle dose of firmness and honesty from her seems to surprise him. (She surprises herself.) He sits back in his chair, listens, and remains calm.

She emphasizes they've yet to hear back from Damian, who may, just may, choose to revise his appraisal. Yet they can't depend on that. For now they have to go with what they have.

Max asks to let him think it over. When she has more information, he'll decide.

Good enough. Not really the answer she wanted, but good enough. At least he didn't freak out. Maybe she's had a good effect on him, helped him improve his personality....

Nah, she reflects as she leaves, *he's only at half-strength. The real Max would've eaten me alive!*

She checks her phone for messages. Nothing today. Nothing from anyone. In real estate this could be a good thing or a bad thing.

An absence of calls can equal no business. It can also equal no disasters. It can also produce anxiety, as in, "Why haven't I heard back from him? Or her? Or those people?"

There's been no reply from Damian, even after Jose sent him comps last night, and she and Kim did the same this morning. His non-response is holding them up. Non-responses are usually bad.

Pulling in to a drive-thru she orders some fast calories. She hates doing it, but she hasn't eaten all day. She's been doing this too much. Everyone at the office does. It seems to be the real estate way.

It's hot and the A/C's blowing. As she waits she thinks about her rejected buyers and the Californians.

Will she ever sell them anything? Will the saddened couple recover? Were the golden state visitors for real? She'll need to follow up with both of them. She can't let them get away. And they could very well "get away" if she's not diligent. She's discovering that clients need to be pursued, chased, hunted, nurtured.

The agent may be the spider and the client the fly, but the agent's web is weak, especially in this modern era of technological choices. The client can easily escape. It's happened to her already twice in her young career. She made mistakes; buyers disappeared. She's in training to fix that and improve, as all agents should continue to do throughout their careers. She's working on her skills, learning how to handle situations—

Ding! A text from Jose.

"Damian isn't changing the appraisal. It's $85K. That's it. How would your buyer like to proceed?"

Lisa tosses her phone on the seat beside her. She needs to eat. She gets her food, then actually goes into the restaurant to sit. Eating in the car is too messy and the office is too far away. It's lunch time.

Time out.

She gives Max another time-out too. She chooses to wait a day to bother him again. Meanwhile his loan is coming along well, according to Olivia. It's already gone into underwriting, the final approval process. If no further paperwork, etc., is required by the underwriter, they're hoping to close early, well before the contract date. But they'll have to get past this appraisal issue first.

Kim and Beth congratulate Lisa on keeping Max in the game. To them, the fact that he has to move due to his rental situation is immaterial. She's kept him in contract mentally. Through the disappointing inspection, the lender arguments, his unexpected illness, and now the appraisal problem, she's kept the deal alive by visiting with him, talking with him, spending time with him.

He could've found a way out. If she appeared uninterested or uncaring, he may have looked for other options and canceled. Her extra effort has made the difference. It's a small deal, yes. Small payday. Some agents might've abandoned it as not important enough to save, not worth their time. But it's big to her, her first real test. She's getting through it. Kim sees this and lets her know she's proud of her. If only all her team agents worked that hard!

They go over the appraisal issue together again like football players in a huddle. Lisa comes out ready for Max.

He doesn't answer, then calls back.

"Whad'ya got?" he asks, sounding stronger.

She runs through the stats: the value stays at $85,000 but the seller wants $88,000 and Max will still get his $1000 repair credit.

"What about eighty-six?" he haggles.

"You're already technically there."

"Come again?"

"You're putting twenty percent down. Twenty percent on $90,000 is $18,000. You already had that eighteen earmarked to spend."

"Yeah?"

"So twenty percent of $85,000 is $17,000. Now put the extra $1000 in, which you were gonna spend anyway, and you're at $86,000."

"So I don't lose anything."

"Right."

"Huh. Sounds good to me."

"Okay, I'll tell them eighty-six."

Lisa goes back to Jose with $86,000. He grunts and sighs and says he'll let her know. A few minutes later it's $87,500 from the seller. Meeting them halfway. No lower.

"Do we still have a repair credit?" she checks to make sure. He confirms it, yes. $500 now, not $1000.

She reports back to Max.

"So I still gotta put in $1500 more?" he grumbles.

"Well, you're getting $500 back, so it's like $1000."

He's quiet, but she can hear him struggling for words on the other end of the phone.

"Look," she says, "what do you want more? What's more important to you? A lower price or a repair credit?"

"The price."

"Then do eighty-seven. They won't give you a credit but I'll get you a home warranty for your repairs."

"How much is that?"

"Around $400-$425."

"Aw Lisa, no, no, you don't have to do that. I can't take your money."

"I'm just trying to get you a deal, Max. You come out of pocket $1000 and I'll put $400 back in. $600 more, that's all it'll cost you extra here."

Again he's quiet.

"Max? You still there?"

"Yeah yeah, I'm here. Aw jeez Lisa, I hate to cost ya 400 bucks like that."

"Okay, well, you think about it." A pause. "You still want the place, right?"

"Yeah, of course!"

"Remember, we got 'em down more than half. They'll go for eighty-seven. I'll pick up the repair cost."

They leave it there.

Lisa goes down to the lunchroom and grabs a bottle of water from the fridge. She feels good but worried. Exhausted, good, and worried. Real estate can be so tenuous. So precarious, like a car hanging off a cliff.

Max calls back. That was fast.

"I'll take it," he growls.

"The eight-seven with the warranty?"

"Yeah, what you said."

Dead deal? No. Deal done.

She revs up, clearing the new price with Jose and the seller, then getting with Beth for a contract price addendum for Max to sign. Beth will order the home warranty as well. They'll get everything over to Olivia and Kendra so they can update their numbers and files. Another hurdle jumped.

Lisa's excited now, yet a slight twinge of worry and caution remains. She knows things can crumble at the last moment. What if Max ends up in the hospital again? Or what if something unexpected comes up and affects his loan? She yearns to know what it feels like to close a property, to actually get it done. She sees her office mates celebrating and high-five-ing whenever it happens. She wants to celebrate and high-five too.

Max needs this, and she needs it too.

To keep her otherwise occupied, Kim hands her a few more buyer leads to chase, along with a business contact looking for an upscale rental. One of her mother's friends contacts her as well, looking to sell her home and purchase another. Wow, a listing! Her first! Suddenly she's busier than she's ever been. She dives in.

The week zips by. She doesn't even take a day off. Though Max fades a bit into the background, she knows he's okay because of updates from Olivia.

He's satisfied with his interest rate but not his lending and title fees. He also doesn't like the quote his insurance guy gave him, so they're trying to find something better. Basically he sounds like his old self again. Lisa is just thankful he's not complaining to her about things she can't control. Instead of a phone call she shoots him an email to check in with him and let him know she's excited they're on their way to closing soon. He replies with a kind thank you for everything she's done for him, and a firm declaration that he'll never use this "horrible" lender again.

Poor Olivia. Again, Max is quite a case.

The only time Lisa gets a taste of Max's excitability is when she sends him his HOA rules and regulations package.

"I'm supposed to read this?" he cries. "It's three hundred pages!"

"Just look through it. Plan to do anything weird with the property?"

"Like what?"

"I don't know. Loud parties? Architectural additions?"

"Hell no."

"Okay. Just hold onto it. In case you ever need it."

"Sure hope I don't."

She hopes so too.

Then she gets a wonderful surprise. The buyers for her rejected buyers' house have backed out. The house is available again. The listing agent wants to know: are her buyers still interested?

She calls them immediately and reaches the wife, who starts to cry again. Of course, of course they're interested!

Just like that, Lisa has her second escrow. Different lender, different title company, same procedure. She glances quickly at her notes. She's got this.

Olivia gets Max's loan paperwork completed and sent to title so he can sign. Beth schedules him an appointment with Kendra.

On the day of the signing, Max meets Lisa first at the house for the final walk-through. This is when the seller signs off on the property and releases the agents and their brokers of any further liability. But few things are this easy with Max.

Still moving about slowly he checks the whole place out with Lisa to be sure that nothing has changed since the inspection.

It's the same. Not any better, not any worse. Vacant and ready for a new owner.

"When are we closing?" he asks.

"Hopefully tomorrow."

"Hopefully?"

"Well, likely. You'll sign today, then wire the rest of your down payment—"

"Can I write a check?"

Lisa freezes. She thinks he can. It worked for the EMD. Still, she tries to discourage him from doing that. "It'll slow things down. Delay your closing."

"Lotta fraud with these electronic wires, that's what I hear. Screw that, I'll do the check. I got time."

She asks him to sign the walk-through form.

"I ain't signing that."

"Why?"

"We ain't closed yet. What if something happens after we leave here?

"It's still the seller's property. He'd be responsible."

"I don't feel too good about that. He's probably already left the county."

"Max, c'mon."

"You let me know when the place is mine, I'll sign it."

They meet later at title. Kendra's assistant Patrice shows them to a little room with a big table and they all sit down. Patrice pulls out a thick stack of paperwork.

"I gotta sign all that?" Max complains.

"Not all of it," Patrice responds softly.

"Well I'm still recovering, I was sick, so I hope you ain't gonna rush me."

"No rush."

Lisa eyes the proceedings carefully, paying full attention to everything. It's her first time in a signing room. Max is full of his customary questions and comments, so the process takes longer than usual and threatens to make Lisa late for her appointment with a new buyer lead.

When it's done they walk out together into warm afternoon shadow. He says he's tired and plans to go to the bank in the morning for the check. She watches him saunter to his car as she walks to hers. She can't believe she's almost finished with him and his file.

What will become of her and Max? Will she hear from him anymore?

She wants to think "yes" and "no" at the same time.

Over the next few days Lisa goes about her work, tending to her various clients, meanwhile keeping in touch with Olivia and Kendra to make sure Max's deal is moving to completion. It's such a whirlwind thing, all the pieces falling into place after the many difficulties that slowed them down. She's seen how an escrow can start fast, hit a lull in the middle, and speed up again at the end. She'll see that many times over and over.

At last word comes from Kendra that she's sending the finished file to the county recorder. In an hour or so the property will be in Max's name and Lisa will have her first closing. She feels electric. Empowered.

There's just one thing left. That walk-through form.

She calls Max to congratulate him on his new home. No answer, so she leaves a message.

She goes to the house and picks up the key from the lockbox, then drives over to Max's and knocks on the door. Again, no answer.

She calls. He doesn't pick up.

She starts to fear he's in the hospital again. He's had another stroke. Or worse.

She returns to her car and just sits there, not knowing what to do. This wasn't supposed to end this way, not on her big day.

Then again, escrows are wild unpredictable beings.

Her phone rings. It's a number she hasn't seen before. A new client maybe? Who knows. She answers.

It's a lady named Sherry from the county recorder's office. There's an angry man's voice in the background. *Max's voice.*

"We have a client of yours here," says Sherry. "Says he no longer wants the property you sold him?"

Max shouts behind her. "Gimme the phone!"

Lisa can't believe what she's hearing. Max gets on the line.

"Lisa! You gotta cancel it, I don't want it! Place is a shit shack! Cancel it and get me my money back!"

She's trembling. "But Max, it's yours now. It already recorded."

"We gotta reverse it."

"That— you can't do that. It's your house now. I have your key. I need you to sign the walk-through form!"

"I'm not signing shit!"

Lisa's done. She's fighting tears. She wants to shout at him for everything he's put her through, but she wisely hangs up and calls Kim.

Kim backs her up. He bought it, it's his. There's no reversing anything. As for the unsigned walk-through, Kim will check with their broker Dan.

Max calls her twice more and leaves angry messages, threatening to sue. She gets back to the office and reports this to Kim. Lisa and Kim go to Dan's office and discuss the situation, and Dan calls Max (from Lisa's phone). He asks him why he didn't sign the walk-through, and Max stupidly says because he wanted to make sure the house closed first.

"So now it's closed," says Dan. "Will you sign the form?"

"No. I don't want the place now."

That's all Dan needs to hear. He tells Max he's sorry he feels that way but that he bought the property fair and square, and that he's now the owner, and that there's nothing else Lisa can do for him. Period.

Dan instructs Lisa to mark the form "Buyer refuses to sign" and to drop off Max's house key at title, where it can be held until he decides to pick it up.

Beth turns in the completed file. The following day, Lisa receives the commission check from her first closing.

It's bittersweet. What a great result from near-disaster!

Ben takes her out to dinner and makes a toast to his successful girlfriend and her burgeoning real estate career. She cries for real this time, but happy tears now.

Never again will Lisa see or hear from Max.

Nor even the Californians for that matter.

THE OTHER SIDE OF UGH

Chances are that if you're reading this book, you're either:

1. *Looking to become an agent*
2. *A newly licensed agent*
3. *An established agent*
4. *Or a consumer curious about what agents do*

There are over 13,000 licensees in Clark County, NV, alone, with more coming. The training classrooms at GLVAR headquarters are always full. It's an incredibly popular field right now. Just as it seems everyone knows an agent, you may know someone just getting into the industry.

If you're one of those about to enter, I hope you've learned something here.

If you're already an agent, I'm sure you feel somewhat validated and yet still have some arguments with me. That's fine.

If you're a consumer - a potential buyer or seller, or just a homeowner, whatever – I do hope I've both educated and enlightened you as to the joys and pitfalls of the real estate lifestyle.

What we do may look easy, and sometimes it is.
Sometimes.
There may be lots of smoke and mirrors behind the often glitzy photos of agents seen on websites, advertisements, and business cards. Basically we're all just entrepreneurs, trying to be successful at our own businesses.

I remember remarking on my first day at the office that I'd never seen so many sharply-dressed and made-up unemployed people in one room.

I've met people who appear jealous of what I do and put it down. Maybe that's because they're unhappy with their own lives and/or jobs. Maybe it's because they'd like to do what I do, but couldn't handle the commission-only, no-weekly-paycheck aspect. Or maybe it's because they know they lack the required people skills and would fail.

One guy told me he thought agents were trained to be a bunch of "weenies". I let it go and didn't bother to ask him what he meant by that, but it's clear he misunderstood what I did each day.

This isn't just selling houses. It's selling yourself. Building a brand. Instilling confidence and trust in others. Making peoples' lives better. Improving your community. Your clients won't be your clients for long if they don't see these qualities in you. Not everyone can do this.

Real estate has to have an effect on you before you can truly have an effect on others.

In the beginning I chose real estate because I wanted the freedom to make my own hours and be my own boss. Not many professions can afford you that. I stay for that very reason. I wouldn't want to do anything else. I like the fact that every day is different. I can always expect the unexpected. Some good, some bad, yes, but rarely dull. I'm learning still. I'll never stop. You won't either.

(If you get to a point where you think you know it all, then you'd better step out.)

In real estate, there's no getting worn down by the bland sameness of the everyday. Each sunrise is a dice roll. You'll have some duties to perform, paperwork to get through. Regular stuff. Then what?

Your phone and inbox are portals of both magic and doom.

Will you be able to catch that curveball from title or will it smack you directly in the nose?

Who sent those flowers, and don't they smell lovely?

If you don't mind surprises, if you dread daily drudgery, this lifestyle may be a great choice for you. I love "going to work" each day. I believe I can handle whatever may come my way. If I can't, I'll have to figure it out. I'll research it or ask a trusted colleague. Perhaps I'll learn something new, which is great. I never run out of things to do, and I never get bored.

The perceived glamour of this way of life, the potential money, the lack of "heavy lifting", they're nice. I won't lie. But there's more than that.

Working in real estate is in essence a way for you to get to know yourself. It's a study in self-examination. And self-preservation. You may not really know yourself fully until you've experienced it. And then you can step back and decide if you like what you see, or if you need to make any changes.

It's self-therapy while practicing therapy on others while trying to make a living off the whims and financial capabilities of mostly relative strangers.

Yes, that's it.

At first I feared it would turn me into one of those money-obsessed zombies I told you about. Instead it turned me into a money-obsessed robot.

No, I'm just kidding.

Actually the changes I've noticed in myself are good.

Before, if something went wrong in my life, I'd be thrown, confused, unsure. I was used to a standard routine, nothing really different happening from day to day. Go to work, come home. Go to work, come home. Very mechanical. If something came along and disturbed that routine, it would bother me. When life is a fairly smooth ocean and then the tsunami comes, you don't know how to react. Now, it may sound funny to hear, I'm conditioned to things going wrong, or potentially going wrong, all the time, as you've seen can happen. So it's okay if the tire goes flat or the water heater blows. I mean, not really okay, but manageable. Life's little doses of adversity no longer seem so scary. While I'm still the perfectionist I've always been, I've discovered that not everything can be perfect all the time.

Real estate will teach you this fast.

It will also teach you that for every down, there's an up.

When my wife and I separated, I was upset, no doubt. I'd never planned on getting divorced. But there I was, on my way. I'd just finished up my first year in real estate. It had been difficult, a very slow rise with several failures thrown in. I was just starting to enjoy my first real taste of success. Now this. My eleven-year marriage and sixteen-year relationship was ending. We had a small child together. I wasn't counting on the breakup of our young family. It shook me.

Though not for long.

The day after my wife moved out, I took a long walk in the open desert behind my neighborhood. At the base of the Nevada Sheep Mountain range I reflected on things, considering the past and the future. It occurred to me that the professional disappointments of the past year had shown me I could take the blows of life, recover, and fight some more. Though I may lose a deal or a client, there'd always be another waiting around the corner. I told myself there would be life beyond this massive personal pothole. I could survive it. And I did.

If that sounds like corny personal psychology, maybe it is. So be it. Some people may not know they have it in them to persevere. Real estate showed me I did. Essentially it was a problem to solve.

I've always enjoyed the challenge of figuring out a problem and coming up with a solution. I prefer professional problems over personal, but hey, you can't always predict what you'll face in life. You can't even predict what you'll face in an escrow! Yet there's always, somehow, an answer. In my work I push myself for answers practically every day. Whether it's negotiating a contract, searching for new leads, looking for buyers for my listings, or helping a buyer with a limited budget in a tight market, I'm constantly flexing my solution-searching muscles.

Before real estate, I never had to do anything like that. I didn't have to be that creative. I only had to show up to work and pick from a list of readily available band-aids to any issue I might face. Along with that I also enjoyed the luxury of guaranteed income. Even if I couldn't fix the problem, no matter what it was, I still got paid. Not so with this gig. I had to learn to push myself further, harder. If I don't, I fail. I fail both myself and my clients. Doing real estate is like going to church every day, and you are your own confessor.

You ask yourself:

"Have I been good? Have I been doing what I can to create and sustain business and keep my clients happy?"

Remember you're your own employer too.

"Would I fire myself for doing a bad job?"

You have to satisfy yourself before you can satisfy others. I truly believe this. I need to feel confidence, stability, in what I'm doing. Otherwise how could I move forward and try to help my clients? If my clients sense I don't have faith in myself, how will they have faith in me? Self-examination for self-preservation. This is a service industry, real estate. It's retail on the highest level.

Retail honed my people skills; real estate sharpened them. I always wanted to see my customers happy. Good service was important to me. It still is. It has to be. And I have to be able to provide it. By doing this I succeed. I've always had a healthy drive to be successful. Real estate only magnified it. I have to be successful, or else.

Like a caveman hunting for food each day – you can laugh, but it's an accurate comparison - there's no choice.

Real estate has done a lot for me.

It exposed a deeper personal strength and confidence I had hiding within. It guided me to a deeper level of problem solving. It taught me that perfectionism is folly. And it intensified my desire to succeed, to survive.

These are big life skills. Some people never acquire them. I bring them now to each and every transaction I have the honor to participate in. My clients can feel that I've been through not only job training but life training. They can sense that I'm worthy of their trust, that I'll do my best to lead them the right way, because I'm confident I can.

When my friend Mark from the drugstore finally comes around and decides to list his house so he can get himself that newer, better one, I'll be ready.

As an agent, it comes down to a basic question:

How can you sell yourself to others if you can't sell yourself to yourself?

ABOUT THE AUTHOR

Bill Giannini lives in Las Vegas, NV, and is a licensed Realtor® with Platinum Real Estate Professionals.

He can be reached at *billgiannini.net*.

www.ingramcontent.com/pod-product-compliance
Lightning Source LLC
Chambersburg PA
CBHW031531210526
45464CB00012B/1916